When Worlds Collide

Published in 2023 by Welford Publishing

Copyright © Amy Fleckney 2023

ISBN: Paperback 978-1-7390970-1-1

Writing mentor: Cassandra Welford

Editor: Christine McPherson

Author photograph © Graham Instral

A catalogue for this book is available from the British Library.

When Worlds Collide

Love + Light
Amy ♡
x
x x

Amy Heckney

Disclaimer

This book is designed to provide helpful information on the subjects discussed. It is general reference information which should not be used to diagnose any medical problem and is not intended as a substitute for consulting with a medical or professional practitioner.

Some names and identifying details have been changed to protect the privacy of the individuals.

To Jasmine

You taught me to be the person I want to be.
You saved me and you made me.
My daughter, my best friend, my everything.

To Reggie

You gave me the honour of becoming a boy mum.
You are the whirlwind in my life that gives me the strength to never give up.
I'm so lucky to be your mum.
My son, my heart, my everything.

To Arabella

You are the light of my life, the sunshine to my days,
and the bravest little soul.

You have completed us in more ways than you could ever know.

My daughter, my bambino, my everything.

Contents

That girl

By *Amy Fleckney*

There was once a little girl who dreamt of a perfect life, success & happiness...

She then went through shit, went through more shit, and as things got harder and darker...

She realised her children became the strength in her heart to keep going...

She realised by creating a vision, a thought, or an idea in her mind, it would become her reality...

She knew it didn't matter how... She trusted it...

Now standing looking out at the sea, the same sea, the same spot she had stood at many times in her life, with so many different thoughts and feelings at different moments.

That same girl, but she had changed, everything had changed. The perfect life for her, the success for her and the happiness for her had slowly become her reality...

You see, no matter what you go through, you will turn the light back on. Your mind is the most powerful tool, and happiness comes in all different ways.

But you will always carry ***that girl*** in your heart.

xxx

Mission Statement

All I ever wanted to do was help people,
Heal some grief in their hearts,
Give them some hope,
And provide for my kids

Xx

4th October, 2016: Lisbon, Portugal

Have you ever had one of those moments when everything feels so perfect that you want to hold it in your heart forever? I was 80 metres above the ground, standing on the viewing platform of the famous Jesus Christ statue overlooking the stunning city of Lisbon. Wow, what a view! For me, this was one of those moments.

The sky was so blue and the sun was beating on my face, which hurt from smiling and laughing so much. From the outside looking in, we seemed like a normal couple in love. Laughing, joking, and holding hands. I loved that feeling; we never went anywhere without holding hands. I never wanted to let go – not now, not ever.

During that special moment and our sacred time away together, it was 'just us'. This was a saying we later adapted to encompass our whole being. A saying we would often repeat to keep the reassurance within our relationship and within our world, which was strange given the irony of our love. In reality, it was never 'just us'. But in that perfect moment, it felt like it was.

As we were standing on the huge statue of Jesus, with his arms spread out blessing the whole of the city, there were a few minutes when everyone on the platform was completely silent. I'm not necessarily a religious person but I felt the silence; it was mesmerising. I was able to feel the butterflies in my tummy fluttering as if they were dancing to the beat of my heart. Yes, it's cheesy, but he was my one and only.

There was nothing this man could do to ever make me stop loving him.

Never in a million years had I imagined that I would fall in love again, but there we were. Together, we stood strong: us against the world. As I looked over the Portuguese city, I felt completely whole. It was as though all the broken pieces in my heart were slowly starting to blend together and repair. I was finally finding who I was again, and I felt alive.

I used to say it was as though I had been dead for years, just going through the motions and existing in my skin. For so long I'd felt like I wasn't living; just coping is the best way to describe it. But in that magical moment, I felt excited for my future and what I would become.

Chapter One

3rd October, 2019

Text to Gemma:

I can feel the panic, I can't breathe, I'm shaking. I can't do this. He is going to tell me he is staying at home. I know it.

I was attempting to get myself ready for bed when she replied. She kept telling me to breathe, but the panic continued to close in around my chest. The room wouldn't stop spinning, and it felt like the air was being sucked out of my lungs whilst I was engulfed in each hideous panic attack. I was losing control, but somehow I got myself sitting on the floor to make sure I didn't pass out.

I was messaging Gemma the whole time, just putting my jumbled words and feelings together, which somehow kept me distracted from the fact I was freaking out. I was terrified, begging her to help me and to take away the physical pain that was shooting through my entire body.

Both my friends, Gemma in Scotland and Kerry in Essex, were listening to me falling apart over WhatsApp. I couldn't move my body without the agonising pain, which was indescribable at this stage.

I was starting to lose the ability to keep going, which was scary. Until now, I had always found a way to put my feelings away in a pocket somewhere during the day. I had my kids to look after, as well as a business to keep going. It was doing so well, but how could I continue to give other people hope and healing when I was completely falling apart myself?

I had reluctantly been back to the doctor for the first time in years to ask for help with my mental health. Five years of highs and lows, a never-ending torment of would it be 'just us' or would there be an ending that I couldn't bear to think about? There were always so many questions, but never any answers. My head continued to spin, and my heart continued to ache.

I was broken.

Until then, I had never considered taking my own life. I had my children, and that's all that I needed to keep me going, but for the first time ever I found myself typing the haunting words:

Kerry, I don't want to live...

I could barely see the words through my tear-soaked eyes, but this didn't stop my head from wanting an answer to the question that continued to spin in my head. *How on earth had my life come to this?*

Despite my personal life falling to pieces, my business as a psychic medium was thriving and my client base was growing by the day. My psychic ability never usually failed me (so long as I listened...), and now more than ever I was using my ability to connect to my psychic intuition and to spirit. I had finally accepted who I was and what I was meant to be doing with my life.

I had previously trained in beauty therapy, which had been enjoyable but never left me feeling fulfilled. However, my new business as a medium gave me a purpose which I loved, as I had always had big dreams and ambitions. I wanted to give my kids a nice life and be able to sleep at night knowing we had food in the cupboards and a roof over our heads. It had taken me years of hard work to even get close to this. But just when things were finally falling into place in my business, they were going to shit elsewhere...

4th October, 2019

He always called me as soon as he could, but today was different. I knew why the phone didn't ring.

I waited until 8am, whilst the kids were getting ready for school, and I had my shower. I was shaking; it was like I was hungover. Everything was an effort, and I could feel my heart and my body growing heavier as I dragged myself around my ensuite in slow motion, trying to gather my messed-up thoughts.

I desperately wanted to take my control back. But the one person I had let into my life and into my heart was tearing me apart. I didn't want to hear the dreaded words I had repeated in my brain come out of his mouth, but they did.

I was clock-watching and still not dressed. Wrapped in a towel, I couldn't wait any longer, so I just took a deep breath and called him. He didn't answer the first time, and it rang out, so I tried again. I realised that I had to take the bull by the horns and accept whatever happened.

My heart was pounding when he answered, but he sounded different. Distant, like a stranger. That only fuelled the dark thoughts that had kept me awake all night, but he seemed really distracted and couldn't seem to give me much of a conversation. I was putting on an act, trying to hide my fears, and performing Amy stepped in – a performance I had somehow adapted over the years to suppress how I was really feeling.

After pressing him to just tell me what was going on, suddenly there it was…

'I can't do it… I can't leave. I won't leave,' he said. 'My kids need me. It's over.'

I couldn't move. I had hundreds of emotions running through me, and I was crying and shouting, 'No, no, no! Don't do this to me!'

I'd spent five years loving him unconditionally whilst continually watching him go home, never asking him for answers or a plan, because I knew he didn't have either. He always looked to tomorrow; that was his attitude.

As a mother myself, I had always understood that his family and children came first. But hearing those haunting words after five years of showing my loyalty to him was just too much to take.

Maybe this day had always been meant to come, but I found myself screaming down the phone. In one breath I was telling him how much I loved him, but in the next I screamed how much he had let me and the kids down, and how I had always thought better of him.

I kept saying he needed to tell me to my face that it was over. But he couldn't, and he didn't. He chose a bloody phone call! I had always stuck by him, supporting him and putting his needs before my own, whilst being open-minded to the situation between us. But this broke my heart.

The next thing I knew, my daughter Jasmine came into my room and said, 'Get dressed, Mum.' I couldn't talk, I couldn't breathe, and I struggled to function.

I couldn't do this on my own. Despite everything I had faced, this was on a whole new level. I knew I couldn't look after the kids properly. I needed to go to my mum and dad's house.

I told Jasmine to get some stuff ready and that we were going to Nanny's. I felt she knew it was bad when I started to get their sleepover stuff ready, but she is such a proactive, empathic child and she asked no questions. She could see I didn't have the answers, and they loved him, too. So much.

And that's what she did. My 11-year-old daughter packed for the family. She was saving me again, but in a different way from before.

I managed to get dressed before dragging myself downstairs, bouncing off the walls as I struggled to walk. My legs felt like they were going to collapse. I picked up the phone and called my parents. 'Dad, I need to come home.' He told me to drive carefully and that they were waiting for me.

Before we left, I called Kerry and began howling down the phone, sobbing. I don't even know if I was talking, but she just kept saying, 'Breathe, breathe, you have to breathe.'

Then I called my auntie. I just wanted someone who understood me to take the knife out of my back; the knife that had been stabbing into my heart and felt twisted and stuck. My auntie has always been a constant support to me with everything I have done in my life. She isn't just my auntie; she's my godmother, my friend, and everything in between.

She arrived on my driveway, saying there was no way she was letting me drive alone all the way to my parents in the state I was in. So we loaded up the children and all their bits, then I followed her on the 50-mile journey to my mum and dad's house.

In all honesty, I don't remember the drive. My body was in physical pain that had been gradually building up throughout the night. I was certain it was closing down on me. I had taken the anti-depressant tablets the doctor had prescribed earlier in the week, so surely I should have felt a bit better? But the pain was unbearable.

I'm not scared of much, but at that moment I was petrified. Would I ever recover? How would I ever get over this? My heart was broken. I couldn't do this again.

Arriving at my parents' house was a blur. The kids ran in as they always did, but once inside, Jasmine hovered around me. She does that when she is worried. She had grown to love 'my partner', and the kids had built a close relationship with him. She trusted him, so this would have been a disappointment to her.

She had never seen us row or be upset, because we never really did. The only thing that ever came between us was *the situation* and *the other life*, but up until then we had always got through it. Well... I always managed to get through it. It was me that had to be strong and deal with what I was involved in. You may have guessed it by now, but yes, I'd become trapped in someone else's marriage. Sometimes I couldn't believe the nightmare that had become my reality.

My auntie stayed with me the whole day whilst I sat silently in my parents' conservatory. I couldn't talk, I had no words, but she held my hand, and I never wanted her to let go. The thought of the pain never leaving was terrifying, and I was shaking the whole time.

My mum was looking after the kids while my dad sat quietly in the front room. When my dad has anything to say, it's always worth listening to. I'm sure he has a sixth sense he just doesn't know about. Every now and then he would pop out to the conservatory to try and get me to eat. Dad is a feeder; no-one goes into his house without having a cup of tea and some sort of food, usually cake! But unfortunately, there was no amount of tea and cake that could help this awful situation. I knew he meant well, but my words still wouldn't come out.

At one point, my dad said, 'If *you* had to make a choice between someone else or your kids, who would *you* choose? He doesn't have a choice, but it will be ok... in time.'

I'm sure my dad thinks I don't listen to him, but I really do. And those words gave me so much hope. If my dad still believed in him somehow, then it had to be okay. Dad was always right (well, most of the time, and let's not make that a big deal, ha, ha!) and I care a lot about his thoughts. It was hard for him, because my 'relationship' went against all his morals and everything he believed in. Actually, you might not believe this, but it went against all of mine, too.

I grew up with the dream of marrying the love of my life and living happily ever after. But nothing had gone to plan, and I hated that my parents had to see me falling apart. After separating from the kids' dad six years before, I always felt like I had let Dad down, but it was a pattern I had repeated growing up, so this felt no different.

My choice of relationship now went against everything he stood for, yet his words brought me some comfort that I hadn't let him down and that he didn't think badly of me. I think he felt genuinely sorry for me. He had raised me to face up to any consequences of my actions, and I guess that was what I was doing the best I could with my broken heart. But the sadness was almost too much to bear. All I could see in front of me was black. The light I always managed to find in life had somehow disappeared. I tried, but this time I just couldn't find the switch.

For hours, I cried, and I sobbed; it was all I could do. Kerry kept messaging my mum to check on me throughout the day, as she was scared for me. She had watched me rebuild my life and raise the kids, riding the rollercoaster I had been on for years. But she was scared because she knew I didn't have any more to give. This had finished me.

Chapter Two

The next day

The following morning, the emotion came in waves. The panic and dread of him not calling me at his usual time of 7.30am on his way to work was unbearable. It had been my wake-up alarm call from him for so long, and I loved this start to the day. Just hearing his voice made me feel so good, and we'd laugh and arrange plans for the week and when we'd see each other. It was all about the simple life and the little opportunities we would have together.

There was so much I'd had to sacrifice. I hadn't been able to share the normal stuff you would expect from a relationship, so the simple things like being able to plan a lunch together kept me going.

But that particular morning, as the time passed with no contact, there was nothing to keep me going with any hope for us.

He wasn't going to call.

Once again, I was alone. Well, that's what it felt like. I couldn't get my head around the fact that he hadn't followed me to my parents' house. The man I knew would never have let me drive all that way in the mess I was in. He knew he had broken my heart, but he was being a coward and couldn't face me. He had convinced himself that the marriage he'd told me he was going to leave one day was now somehow going to be salvageable.

Over the next two days, while I stayed at my parents' house, he promised to give me the explanation I deserved. He knew he was welcome at their home, and he reassured me he would come and visit me whilst I was there.

I'm aware I may not be painting the most desirable picture of, let's call him Mr R, but despite the mess we were in, he isn't a bad person. He had the kindest heart and didn't intentionally set out to hurt anyone. Somehow, he had managed to juggle everything whilst thinking he was pleasing everyone.

I had been in such a vulnerable place when we first met, and he was the one who had given me a feeling of security. I honestly, hand on heart, felt he would never let me down – or not intentionally, anyway. But in that time of despair, all my sympathy for him had run out. I needed him to see with his own eyes how much of a mess his web of lies had got us all in.

The only thing that got me through those tortuous few days was the hope that every time my phone went off it could be him. I was a bag of nerves.

Sadly, I had given my power away through the emotional pain I was enduring, and I was devastated. For the first time ever, I felt like an outsider – the actual third person that I had always known I was. But knowing and feeling are two totally different things.

I understand the hurt our relationship would cause. This was real-life shit. Lives were getting ruined, and hearts were being broken. I could see he was losing control and felt completely out of his depth.

He was being pulled from pillar to post. I wanted him, and they wanted him. My kids needed him, too. Not for security or financial gain, but because they loved him. He was torn between two worlds that had collided, and it was no wonder he was falling apart. But that still didn't change the fact that he wasn't able to give me the time I deserved just to talk.

I knew I was mentally ill, but I just didn't know how I was going to move forward. My good friend Jenny had said to me in a message:

Keep it simple and just focus on breathing.

It was probably the best advice anyone could have given me at this point.

I arrived home from my parents' house a few days later, as the kids had to get back to school and I needed to just get through each day, one breath at a time. Mr R was still avoiding seeing or talking to me, but I knew he was being monitored at all times and watched like a hawk.

During this time of not having contact, I made a decision that no matter what, I was going to stand by him. You're probably thinking, *Noooooo!* But deep within the darkness, I still loved him and believed in us. Even if it took more years and more heartache, I was going to do it.

As you can imagine, not everyone supported me with this choice. Thankfully, though, my 'Table for Four' girls understood. They were the friends that I would go 'out out' with.

They were expecting me on a night out that very evening, so I had to message and say: *Sorry, girls, I can't come out tonight as planned. Mr R has chosen to stay at home, we are over. I'm broken. I can't talk about it. For now I need to get well.*

This was one of many similar messages I had to send to my closest friends, the ones who had watched my heart break and be torn. The ones who had all welcomed Mr R into our circle of trust. Although they knew he was married, they never treated him any differently to a normal boyfriend. They all adored him – as did my parents, my auntie, and everyone who ever met him. It goes without saying that they didn't like what his other life was doing to me and the effect it was having on my wellbeing, but they knew I would stand by him. They knew I had to stick to my gut feeling that somehow, some way, we would make it.

Despite how much my friends liked him, no-one really believed in him. They knew he had too much to lose by leaving his marriage, and deep down they all thought he was a coward. They always told me, 'He won't leave her. He won't tell the truth.' All the usual married-men-having-an-affair comments. If I had a pound for every time someone said he was 'having his cake and eating it', I would have been filthy fucking rich!

But the one thing no-one close to us ever questioned was how much he loved me. That was crystal clear to see.

I didn't know how we would ever be together, only that we couldn't be apart. I had to be the strong one to make the right choices for us. His life as he knew it was over; the life I had been used to for the last five years was over. I didn't know at this point how I was going to move forward; being without Mr R wasn't an option. But I realised I had to respect his choice for now and just keep believing in our love, friendship, and the soul mate connection we had.

My friend Sally was the only one who told me to wait for him. And by this she meant no matter what it took. She said to me, 'You're going to stand by him, aren't you? Even though he has proved everyone right by not choosing you, I know you're going to stand by him, and I will stand by you.' This was all I needed to hear. It was such a comfort knowing that someone understood me and my reasoning. Again, I know it sounds so cheesy, but I just couldn't be without him. It just *had* to be okay.

The following week was a mess. After the morning school run, I would drive 20 miles to Essex from Hertfordshire to spend the days with Kerry, where she'd let me cry, vent, or be silent, but she never left me alone. Being on my own made me pine for him so much. Kerry wanted me to let go of him, and told me that torturing me for five years was enough. But that wasn't about her hating Mr R; it was about the care she had for me. She championed me all the time, always reminding me of how far I had come in my life, my kids, my living situation, and my business, which at that stage still wasn't being affected.

Chapter Three

Twelve days later, I still hadn't seen Mr R. This was the longest I had gone without seeing him or having a proper conversation with him. He would call me for two minutes and ask how we all were, so it was clear he still cared in his own way.

I would ask him, 'Do you love me?' And he would say it wasn't about that any more – but it had always just been about the fact we loved each other so much. That doesn't just stop, and this is what was killing me. Had the whole thing been a lie? No way! Surely I wasn't that stupid? But I felt like an idiot. I felt like he had fooled everyone, including me.

The trust he had broken made me feel worthless. He was the person who would never let me go to a doctor because he would help me face my anxiety and panic attacks that returned every now and then from previous mental health battles; the person who would listen to my plans, my hopes, and my dreams; the person who believed in me and my ambitions – something I had never experienced before. But now he was like a stranger, happy to watch me lean on my friends for support. Out of sight, out of mind.

At times I would get so angry that I would be screaming into my pillow at night, crying at how stupid I had been to think this situation would ever end well for me! Google became somewhere I would endlessly search for answers, as there had to be someone who could tell me this was going to be ok; someone who had experience of what I was going through.

But during my online searches I couldn't find a single person who wasn't saying 'STAY AWAY FROM MARRIED MEN' and 'don't expect it to end well for the *mistress*' – a word I hated. Those kinds of comments weren't helping at all. If anything, they were making me feel a piece of shit.

Last time I'd felt low and needed answers, I had begged for a sign or some guidance from my nan, who is in spirit. In her own way she had shown me the way to Mr R, and in all my years of connecting to spirit I had always trusted they would guide me. Now, though, I wasn't getting clear guidance.

Everything was a mess.

During the weekend, I spent time with my friend Elaine. The kids played happily, and she just allowed me to be still and silent, which became my way of just processing the moments. She also gave me comfort by reassuring me that this couldn't be the end of me and Mr R. She was another friend who had stood by us and watched us grow – the kids and I were so lucky to have all these amazing women around us.

During that Saturday he called me. It took me by surprise that it was a FaceTime call, and I could see he was still at work. He promised he would come and see me on Monday for us to talk and clear the air, and for the first time in a week he told me he loved me. He almost seemed back to normal, and I could see glimpses of Mr R again, which lifted my spirits and gave me what I needed to get through the weekend. Jasmine was staying at Elaine's for the night, so I knew I would go back there on Sunday to collect her, then all I had to do was get through the night. Monday would be there before I knew it, and he'd promised we could talk properly.

I could do this.

I was so lucky to have such good friends, and I know that I would have sunk without them at that time. Their constant messages to check on me were like comforting hugs.

Monday morning came, and the kids went off to school. Waiting to hear from him, I felt sick to the pit of my stomach. I knew I couldn't go to his work because everything he did was being monitored. But I just couldn't sit and wait for him to call.

Somehow, I found the strength to start driving to his work. I was determined this mess needed to be sorted out. On my way there, I called him, but there was no answer. I kept calling. No answer. What the hell was going on?

On the third call, he finally answered, and I knew straight away he wasn't there; the background didn't sound right. My stomach lurched with dread and fear, and all the feelings of that dreadful morning two weeks before began to come back. Despite the panic, I tried to act normally and managed to say, 'What time are we meeting?'

He replied, 'Not today…'

I was so angry. My blood was boiling, and I was literally shaking again. All weekend I had clung to his promise to see me and talk to me, to give me some sort of explanation as to how the hell we were going to get through this… because that's just what we did. It's what we had always done for five bloody years!

During this whole crappy mess, I had always accepted in my head that his life with his family came first and that this day might come, but my heart just couldn't accept it. However, I wasn't forcing him to leave them or to change his mind. I just wanted an explanation, which I felt he owed me. We had supported each other for five inseparable years. So, to think I was going to say ok and be silent to make it easier for him – like I had done for the whole duration of our relationship – was not on. I absolutely couldn't do that.

It was my turn to talk; it was my turn to be able to make some conditions, seeing as there had never been any. But my unconditional love for him never left me, no matter how painful and tormented I felt. And that is exactly what it was – utter torment. And the more he avoided me, the more tortured I felt. I had a flashback from a psychic reading from two years before when I'd been told that this relationship would result in one big ball of pain.

I'm not a needy person, as I have spent too much time alone, but this situation fucked my head up so much. As I was driving, I kept shouting, 'What! What? Not today?' I kept repeating, 'I have waited. I'm falling apart! I'm trying to raise the kids whilst being tortured by this mess!' I hated shouting, and I knew he hated being shouted at, but I needed answers.

In the heat of the moment, I said, 'I'm coming to see you anyway, so you will have to talk to me. This can't go on, as it's not fair. It's all so unfair.'

There was a brief pause, and then his reply took the air from my lungs, and it felt like time stood still. I felt the life drain from me once more as he said quietly, 'I'm not there.'

I said, 'Where the fuck are you? Where could you possibly be at a time like this?'

Just 48 hours earlier he had FaceTimed me and given me hope of some time to talk… But the reality was that when we spoke on that FaceTime call, he had been leaving work and was moments away from jumping on a plane with his mates! He had chosen to hide that from me, pretending that we were going to meet on Monday.

In all honesty, I wouldn't have had a problem with him taking some time out. But the fact that he didn't tell me the truth was so disappointing, considering how strong our communication had always been.

He just wasn't a go-away-with-the-boys type. Any free time he had was always shared with me, as our time together was so limited – or he worked. He loved being at work.

At that moment, listening on the other end of that call when he told me he was away, I just felt as though I didn't know him any more. I had lost the man I knew, the one I had fallen in love with, the one I trusted!

But when I screamed back, 'So where the hell are you?' there was one more knife twist to come.

'I'm in Lisbon, Portugal,' he replied.

The place where we had created magical memories. The place where I had felt whole, strong, and secure, a special place where we had created such wonderful memories…

He didn't know when he was going to be back, he said, and then tried to ask about the kids, but I was in no mood to humour him.

'You don't give a fuck,' I spat back, 'so please don't even pretend.'

I could no longer hold back the tears. He had betrayed me so much by fucking off and lying to me. I knew then that I had lost him, and it was over.

It appeared he had finally set me free.

Maybe I was never meant to be trapped in his marriage or trapped in his web of lies. But I didn't feel free; I just felt twisting, horrible, terrible pain.

Chapter Four

I called Kerry whilst I was still driving. She and her husband, who is a great guy, own a menswear shop, and I knew I'd feel safe there. Thinking back, I don't even know what I said to her on the phone, I just know I was sobbing uncontrollably. She just told me, 'Get to the shop. Breathe and get here.'

On my drive there, I let Gemma know what was going on, too. She just wanted me to pack a bag and go to her in Scotland, but taking my kids out of school wasn't an option. Despite my grief and heartache, I couldn't do that to them. They needed normality, and even during all the hardship in the past with their dad, I had always tried to keep things as normal as I could for them. It had to be the same this time.

Arriving at Kerry's shop, I didn't know what to do with myself. She took me through to the back of the shop, and I just remember my legs barely being able to hold me. Finally, I fell into her arms and could smell the washing powder on her clothes; I was that close. She held me, she carried me, and my heart broke in two.

She told me, 'I don't know what to do… you're scaring me. I'm watching parts of you die right in front of me.'

And it did feel exactly like a part of me had died – the result of the emotional torture of five years of loving someone who lived a whole other life.

When I managed to stop crying, I called my parents and told them he had gone. I didn't have to say anything else. My dad simply replied, 'Mum is packing a bag and she is coming to stay.' And that's all I needed to hear. I needed my mum to come and look after me, and that's what she did. I couldn't do this on my own any longer.

Mum always had a way of not asking questions when she knew I didn't have the answers. But I could tell from her face that she knew something was seriously wrong when she walked into my house later that day. The curtains in every room were closed, the house was dark and gloomy, and the bin was full and overflowing. The cushions on the sofa were out of place from where I had dragged the spare duvet downstairs and chucked it on the sofa. It was a way of just feeling warm at night, but I hadn't slept since this downward spiral began.

Instead, I had returned to my safe place, the place where I felt at 'home', which was with Jasmine in her bed.

My son Reggie was seven, so I explained it by saying we were having film nights in Jasmine's room, so he was in there, too. Being together in one room was how it had been when I was living with Jasmine and Reggie's dad – a place to stay safe when he was being irrational, drunk, and verbally abusive.

To Mum, my house looking like a shithole was a massive sign that I was falling apart, because I'm very houseproud, and it's always clean and tidy. My dad is spotless in everything he does, so growing up we always had chores to do, and our whole day was structured by housework. It did my head in at the time; imagine at 12 years old, dusting and polishing door handles as my job every morning. Yes, it was tedious, but it did give me time to imagine my future life – something I always did from such a young age. My visions were always big and ambitious, and I believed then that I could be anything I wanted to be. I always wanted to make a difference in the world.

I believe this is what sparked my childhood desire to join the Army. I used to imagine marching with my team, making a difference, imagining the look on my dad's face during the Remembrance Day marching parade. For years, it was what I really wanted to do. I wanted to make him proud so that he could think, *That's my daughter...*

As you will have realised, I clearly didn't join the Army. Instead, I followed another path – a path I can see now was always meant to happen, but a tough one, nevertheless.

Let me take you back...

When I left school, I went to Sixth Form for a while, because I had been advised by the Army careers office that with A levels I could enter at a more senior officer position, and my GCSE results meant I could have this opportunity. But I felt completely lost and it didn't feel right for me at all, as I was struggling to find my place and where I fitted with it. I enjoyed my subjects, but even my friendship groups started to break down. After being such a popular person throughout my whole school life, I felt I had no friends in Sixth Form. I felt left out, lost my direction, and pulled out after eight months.

My boyfriend at the time begged me not to go to the Army. We had been together for two years by that stage, having met at school. He had left to work full time in a shoe repair shop where he'd had a Saturday job for years, and his ambition was that one day he might take over the shop. He was determined that he didn't want me to go to the Army, and the thought of being away from him was hard and upsetting for me, too, but until then the Army had been all I had ever wanted, so I had no clue what else I could do. To be honest, I have always had a secret deep regret that I never joined the Army, and I felt so lost for years, wondering who the fuck I was or who I wanted to be, because I'd had that vision of joining up for so long.

I always got my nails done regularly in a local salon, and one day they mentioned during an appointment that they needed a full-time apprentice who could learn and work at the same time. I put myself forward for it, and that's how my journey into the beauty industry began. My Army dreams were pushed aside as I went to college in the evenings to learn each module, while by day I was a nail technician in the salon. I loved the job, the people I worked with became my friends, and my high school sweetheart was happy that I had decided not to join the Army. But our relationship only survived another year before we split up, which was when I encountered my first battle with my mental health.

My time in the salon wasn't like going to work; it was so easy, fun, and I loved my days working in Flash Nail Designs... until my 5th year of working there when the owner decided to close the salon. It was a sad time, and I was back being lost with where my life was heading career-wise.

Then I met the kids' dad...

I lived in Bedfordshire, and he lived in Essex. It was love at first sight when we met at a music weekender. Although I was only 20, and there was a 16-year age gap between us, we shared a love for music and dancing, and on our first date we went to a club near where I lived and didn't stop talking for the whole night. We talked a lot, exchanged calls and messages every day when we were apart, and he was so romantic. He even flew me away for a surprise holiday when I turned 21, which was an incredible gift when we had only met three months before. I often wonder if things would have turned out differently with our relationship if I had been much older when we met, but I was young and still lived with my parents. He was amazing at the gifts and the romance in the early stages of our relationship, but did he ever listen to me with what I wanted for our future? No.

I moved to Essex to live with him nine months after we met, and for almost a year I travelled from there every day to a salon in Milton Keynes. He was London born and raised, and I was obsessed with his knowledge of the city I love so much. When I was growing up, my only opportunity to visit London was on the odd school trip, so meeting him opened up such wonderful experiences.

Looking back, though, even then all our dates were his choice, all our trips were his choice, and when I eventually left my job in Milton Keynes, he didn't consider supporting me to set up my own salon — something I longed for. Reluctantly, I accepted a night shift in a local supermarket stacking shelves. Admittedly, it was better money than I would have earned doing beauty treatments, but it gave me my first taste of feeling like I wasn't good enough.

Back in my house looking like a shit tip. With Mum there to help, the following days were up and down. She made dinners for us, helped with the kids, and tried to get me to eat, but I couldn't face it.

All I could think about was Mr R just giving me the time I deserved to clear the air. I was convinced that once that happened, we would find a way to get through this. I had dealt with worse situations in my life, but now I felt done, frustrated, and just couldn't take any more. I needed so much help to piece my broken heart back together.

For a while I had been following an Unconscious Mind Therapist on social media. UMT is a productive talk therapy that aims to resolve the problem that's holding you back in your life, focusing on the recovery rather than the content of the issue, finding resolutions to move forward, and providing you with the tools to do so whilst incorporating hypnosis, if need be. Ultimately it gives you a mindset that lasts for a lifetime. UMT can help you to change past thoughts, feelings, limiting beliefs, and patterns, and is different from most other therapies. The results are instantaneous, and you can feel the positive effects from the very first session.

That sounded like what I needed — and I needed it NOW!

The anxiety and panic attacks I had been feeling were growing worse, and I desperately needed help. These anxiety issues weren't new for me. They had started when I was about 18 and crept back in during challenging times in my life, but usually I somehow managed to keep pushing them to the side and get through each day. Mr R had also helped me; his support over the last few years had without a doubt played a huge role in my healing.

But this time I knew I needed more help. I didn't want to be on medication, as it made me feel as if I was rewinding my progress from the past, so I took the opportunity to message the Unconscious Mind therapist and arranged an appointment whilst my mum could look after the kids.

It wasn't cheap, but nothing worth having is. Since the Mr R situation had caused me so much anguish, I hadn't been able to work to my full potential. But I knew the UMT would be valuable, so I used the last bit of money I had at that time to make sure I could get the therapy I needed.

Thank goodness I did...

Chapter Five

The day that changed everything

I felt really nervous on the long drive to the session. I had no idea what to expect, and I had no clue what the therapist would be like. I kind of hoped he would just magically help me not to love Mr R any more, and cure me from anxiety and depression. But common sense would tell anyone that wasn't likely to be the case.

Butterflies in my tummy were building. and I trusted this was a good thing. Anticipation and anxiety are two very different things, and I was borderline both. I knew just from my gut feeling that this therapy was going to be good for me and that somehow it would work. It *had* to work.

As I was waiting to be called in for the appointment, I was messaging Gemma, asking her to outline what my problems were. I wanted to know how I had got to this point of despair. It sounds crazy, but I just didn't know where to start explaining it to the therapist, and she had been through this with me, always on the other end of a message, so I felt she knew what I needed better than I did.

I had been at my rawest with her through messages at times when I could barely string two words together, so I knew she would be able to be honest with how shit I'd been.

I couldn't think straight, and I was starting to feel sweaty and slightly embarrassed that I was going to have to tell a complete stranger that I had been in a long relationship with a married man who was living a double life. I felt like a fool for ever believing in Mr R, and annoyed that I could be perceived as a home-wrecker. I absolutely am not! Never once did I ever take my role in his double life as a joyride or light-hearted fun. I felt so sad for us all, including his family, for so many reasons. Like me, they were tangled in the web of lies.

I had always known and accepted that his family had to come first, but I wasn't going to hide the fact that I was hurting. I'm not a horrible person, and that's the reason I believe that I took on all of the emotions for everyone involved.

While I waited in a bar area, I was fidgeting about and messing with my clothes, having one of those do-I-leave-my-coat-on-or-take-it-off moments. Let's face it, whether I was wearing a coat or not really didn't matter, but I didn't know what to do for the best! I was faffing.

Gemma was typing for ages and that was making me nervous, but eventually this was her reply:

You go through a range of emotions. You go through severe anxiety attacks which start with your body tingling but result in difficulty breathing, hyperventilating, crippling stomach pains, and all-over body aches.

Mentally, you are all over the place. At your worst, you are very paranoid, question everything, and cry. You don't eat because you physically can't bring yourself to do it. You are very difficult to talk to at your worst; it is impossible to get through to you. You get very fixated and it's very similar to OCD. Repetitive behaviour, needing constant reassurance. Not saying all this to upset you, but it's all true.

I was shocked by her reply. Seeing it in writing showed me how bad my mental health had become. But she was right…

Moments later, the therapist was finally there to take me to the appointment, and I was shocked at how normal he was – relatable and down-to-earth, thank God. I noticed his trainers and his casual approach. This was what I needed, not a man in a white coat judging me; just a normal bloke who would take what I said and help me.

During the session I was waiting for him to almost put me to sleep, like you see on TV when people are under hypnosis. And he did incorporate some hypnosis into the session, but I was awake the whole time. In fact, he got me talking more about me than the situation with Mr R and my past. He asked me questions about my work, my ambitions, my plans (if any), and the main words: 'the visions'. He used UMT to get me talking and tap into what Amy Fleckney was really about, which felt good, because to be honest I had almost forgotten.

I had started my business 18 months prior to the appointment, so when he asked me what I did for a living, I proudly told him, 'I'm a psychic medium.' The therapist was blown away and could see the potential in me that had got lost in all my current mess.

During the session, I surprised myself where I saw my future, how I saw it, and who was in it. One thing that stayed the same was my purpose to be the best mum and medium I could be, and to take my business to the top. Back to being that little girl with big dreams!

He asked me what I wanted next for my business, and I explained how I had wanted to do platform mediumship in a show environment, with a full audience. At that moment, I was thinking it was just a vision. In my eyes, Mr R had been the one to help me push forward, chase my dreams, and make things happen. He had always supported my ambition to succeed, but now that he wasn't around, what would I do? On the other hand, for years I had been raising my children alone, creating the success of my business at a time when shit was being thrown at me left, right, and centre. So really, I could do anything and be anything, with or without his help. That invaluable session taught me to realise that I had so much more to give and so much more to offer than I had ever given myself credit for.

During the treatment, the therapist told me that he was doing a charity hypnosis show the following month, and as our three-hour session drew to a close, he literally threw out to me, 'Why don't you come to my show and perform your mediumship?'

I was stunned. He was offering me an amazing opportunity, a lifeline, so that I had something to focus on other than Mr R. And my God, I grabbed it with both hands and without hesitation said, 'I'm there. I'll do it!'

I left the therapist's room that day with a different mindset: same vision but clearer, and an opportunity under my belt that was going to start bringing it to reality.

Before I headed home, we did some promotion pics on the grounds of the country club where his practice was based, and they were on social media that very day! I had created a vision, and it was actually happening!

I realised I had to get on with my life without Mr R and make plans; he had made his by choosing to stay at home. I wasn't going to lose who I was, as I had too much to give. I still loved Mr R, but my unconscious mind had to accept that the only person who could free me was *me*!

The tools I learnt that day changed my life! The knots in my tummy had untied; it was all in my mindset! And the UMT session taught me that mindset is everything. I had always been a firm believer in the law of attraction, but this felt so different and much deeper. This was about the visions in my mind becoming the reality in my hand!

I now knew that the science behind the power of the mind was true.

I had gone into that room as one person, and left as someone else – someone who felt back in control again; someone who recognised all the amazing things they had to offer. I felt like I had so much to live for again, other than my children and the mental health battle I kept having to face.

I hadn't eaten in a good week, perhaps longer – not properly anyway. But the message I sent to Gemma on my way home was: *I have eaten a whole sandwich and a packet of crisps. I'm starving!*

For days afterwards, I was on a high and kept asking Gemma if she'd noticed a change in me. She told me I wasn't as obsessed, I had stopped fixating, and I was in control of my thoughts and feelings. Again, she was right.

I disposed of the anti-depressants the doctor had given me (please don't follow my example, and seek medical assistance before coming off any tablets), and I made my mum video it so I could remind myself how far I had come. I knew I still had a long way to go, though. Anxiety, depression, and heartache don't just go away, but I have the tools now to move forward and get through each day.

Every morning and every night, I was to take some time to create my visions, set my intentions to the universe, and be clear that what I gave out I would get back. It was a tough thing for me to keep battling with my brain, when at times it would take me to the heartache and thoughts of Mr R moving on with his life.

But right then what mattered was to concentrate on my visions and reinforcing the techniques I had learnt during my UMT session. Mr R would follow and catch up; this was all part of my vision.

I still desperately wanted to be with him. and I knew we could be happy, as we had come this far. But it was vital that my visions and my mindset weren't just based on him and our relationship. They also had to be about me, my life, and the life I was creating. If that meant being without him and continuing to raise the kids alone, so be it. At least I would be free.

So many people in my position as the third person don't get a happy ending. When you're part of a double life – an affair, if you want to call it that – being the other women rarely ends well. But this whole situation had torn me to shreds.

To the outside world, Mr R and his family may have been perceived as the 'ideal family' and had it all – the cars, designer clothes, and a beautiful home.

Which I found quite intimidating. But it's so easy to cast judgement when you don't know the full story. Nothing is quite what it seems, and you can never assume anything.

I'm sure some people thought I was only after Mr R for his money. But if I had been that desperate for a luxury lifestyle, surely I wouldn't have left my ex with just two young kids and literally the clothes on my back? Surely I would have searched for someone to support my needs financially rather than struggling to make ends meet for the years after leaving the kids' dad?

When you know you're second in a line of people that *have* to come first, when you're loyal to someone who can never show that back and yet you remain faithful and supportive, believe me it's not the easy option. And it's definitely not about money. There is no price on that.

Chapter Six

One of the hardest things for me was knowing that someone you love can be intimate with someone else. Of course I knew it had to happen, but it rips at your self-respect and dignity. I often wonder now if I thought that little of myself. Was my opinion of myself that low.

It was a topic Mr R and I tried not to talk about. The performance side of me would come into play again, where I would have to ignore it and squash it away somewhere in my brain. But at times it would drive me insane. My imagination would run wild, but I chose to deal with it the best way I could. Don't ask me how because I don't know how; I just compartmentalised this topic. He avoided any of my questions on it and would shut me out of any discussion on the subject.

I wanted to do the right thing and cut ties, and I wished he could have made his choice and stuck to it. For so many years I had told him to go home, sort his shit out, and come back to me when he was ready. But it was like an undeniable bond that couldn't be broken.

The more pain I felt, the more I loved him unconditionally. I'm aware it sounds ridiculous and know it was a very unhealthy obsession, but when it came down to it, it was just love. Simple. But it really wasn't simple, was it? The one thing that couldn't change was our love, but I had to change the way I dealt with it.

During the week that followed the therapy, I was finally able to come face-to-face with Mr R. Our much-anticipated meeting ended up being in a roadside lay-by as he made his way back from the airport after his Portugal trip. I was still hurting, but since the therapy I had turned this hurt into the attitude of 'I'm doing me'. I had accepted that he clearly wasn't thinking straight and things had got too much. He just couldn't face all the shit.

As he got into my car, I could tell he knew just by the way I approached him that something had changed within me. I had been given the tools to create my visions, keep my head in a strong position of control, and not allow fear to stop me moving forward. And he could see that I wasn't going to put my life on hold any more. I had made the decision to stand by his choice, but I was determined I was going to live and move forward whilst he did what he needed to do.

I had been through too much in my past to let this bring me down any more. I was in a much better position now – my business was growing, my finances were stable, and my home was secure. So, I didn't have to rely on anyone. I had realised that what I had always wanted and visualised had finally come to fruition – to provide for the kids by myself, keep a roof over our heads, and be able to sleep at night. The vision I created all those years back had come to reality. When you believe, you will receive.

In the car with Mr R, he didn't say much. I was looking for reassurance that there was still love, which meant there was hope and that he wasn't going to just vanish from my kids' lives. They deserved so much better than that. They had grown to love and respect him, and they trusted him. I had never let them build this bond with anyone else, as I had always been so protective.

But he kept repeating how things were never going to work, we wouldn't get any time together, and that he couldn't breathe at home without being asked a million questions. He didn't cope well under pressure.

I don't even remember how things were left that night. It was so late and dark. Sitting in the car, not really getting anywhere with how this mess was going to become even a tiny bit clearer, was enough to make anyone go batshit crazy.

But for the first time in a while, I felt in control of my emotions.

I felt so much better seeing him, and I knew he loved me. Just from being in his energy, something settled inside me for knowing that, but I also had this whole new outlook on my life – the life of Amy Fleckney. The visions I was creating and the thoughts I was giving out had totally changed.

I told him about the upcoming show with the UMT therapist, and he was happy for me. He always wanted me to succeed, but I could see he was apprehensive that I was growing. I had work to be done creating my visions and making them happen, and my main vision was that I would do the show and smash it with a successful night of live mediumship.

For my part, I absolutely never set out to cause harm. My parents have been married over 40 years, so I didn't wake up one day and think, *I'm going to fall in love with a married man.*

I felt disappointed in myself most of the time, even though I was trying to be the honest one in the whole tangled situation. But now I realised I could wallow in self-pity, or I could endeavour to keep building my life. And the opportunity to stand on a stage proudly as a psychic medium was going to be the first step on that path.

Chapter Seven

I always knew I could connect to spirit growing up as I'd had dream visitations from passed-over relatives as a child, and unique experiences when my intuition had been always on point. When I was twelve years old, I even had a beautiful set of angel cards, so it was a subject that always interested me. But looking back, I can see that I had to accept this 'gift' when I was ready, and when spirit trusted me to carry out their work. It's a huge responsibility, and I take my role as a medium very seriously with the accuracy of my guidance and messages. So, I'm sure they knew in the spirit world when I would be able to do my best.

My nan passing away in 2007 had a huge impact on the 'spiritual side' of me. I call it that, but the spiritual side is actually just me being me.

Like most of my relatives, I felt I lost part of myself when she passed, as she had been the queen of our family. As I grew up, she lived opposite us, always came on holiday with us, and I saw her every day when I lived with my parents.

Every Wednesday, I would go to her house for my tea of egg, bacon, and homemade chips – a ritual that started from a young age when I used to go to Brownie Guides, and carried on until I left home at the age of 20!

We would chat and laugh while we ate, and afterwards she would nod off watching tv whilst I would sit next to her, just happy to be in her company. Then she would do that classic Nan thing where she would stand at the front door and wave until I reached home, and I would turn for a final wave just before she was out of sight. Our homes were in a cul-de-sac, so when I reached my mum and dad's house, I could see her turn off her outside light – and that was another Wednesday over.

I'm so thankful I spent those times with her, and the precious memories are something that I hold dear in my heart.

September 28th, 2007

Nan was 88, but still full of life, so independent, and well. She would suck a throat sweet each morning and had a theory that this kept all colds and the flu away! I can smell the blackcurrant flavour now as I write this.

That September morning, I had come to my parents' house as I was meeting up with some friends to go off on a girls' weekend. I was 21, and living in Essex, but we agreed I would come and pick the others up at my parents' house in Bedfordshire. As always, I wanted to see Nan when I was there.

I knocked on her door but there was no answer. I knocked again; still nothing. Usually, I would hear her radio on, or she would shout, 'I'm coming.' She was so heavy-footed that there was a spot in her living room she would stand on and you could hear it vibrate on the floorboards! But that day, there was no noise, and she didn't come.

I rang my dad as I stood on her doorstep. I didn't want to leave just in case she came, but deep down I knew she wouldn't. How did I know? I knew because I could feel it in my body, and my psychic intuition kicked in. Even though I wasn't a practising medium at that stage in my life, I still 'had it'.

Dad came over and opened Nan's front door with his spare key, but the security chain was still in place on the other side, which meant she hadn't got up to follow her usual morning routine.

Without another word, my dad burst the door in. He knew.

I could tell from his face the sheer panic he must have been feeling; I felt it from us both. It was running through my veins like fire, and I was shaking and trembling as he ran in first and I followed.

I don't remember feeling anything but slow-motion numbness, like nothing I had ever felt before. There she was, lying motionless on her kitchen floor. She looked rested. She didn't look hurt, and she didn't even look like she had fallen over. It was as though she had been gently placed, as if someone had carefully laid her down…

My dad told me to call 999, but I knew she had gone. He sobbed, bent down with her head in his lap, and he just cried.

Dad and I had had quite a volatile relationship at times. I always felt I let him down, but I was annoying when I was growing up. I didn't listen, and I always knew best, which aggravated him a lot. I just couldn't be told; my brain didn't stop, and I always had an answer, so it's no wonder I was so bloody annoying.

I always felt like I was trapped inside my body, full of restlessness and irritation, pure drive and ambition.

I didn't make great choices growing up, either. I would do stupid things and I expect I probably looked selfish most of the time and careless. Looking back, it's because I always chose to ignore my intuition and my spiritual guides. If I had listened back then, would I be who I am now? I'm not so sure.

Spirit knew what was right for me even when I was mid-flow of making a bad choice, for example when I was spending money like it was going out of fashion at the age of 18. I had credit cards that were mounting, and my gut feeling, which we all have, my higher intuition, my ability to be psychic, always kept saying, 'Stop!' But I didn't. So, I learned the hard lesson when I was fucking things up.

That morning in my nan's kitchen, I was eight weeks pregnant with Jasmine (although no-one knew about the pregnancy at that time). And there I was being the shoulder and strength my dad needed. At that moment it was just me and Dad.

The 999 guy was telling me to talk my dad through CPR, so there was Dad trying to revive her, but he was freaking out, begging Nan to come back to us. I kept saying to the guy on the phone, 'Don't let him do this. She has gone.'

I had never seen a dead body before, but I sat down on the floor next to her and told Dad gently, 'She is with Grandad now.' And I meant it. I knew it, and I saw it, like an angel. My nan and grandad were helping me to support my dad, and I know the words came from a higher place than me.

I then had the horrible job of delivering the news to my mum, my auntie, and my uncle, who came as soon as they could.

My dad's brother, Uncle Gig, held my hand whilst I held my nan's, but it felt really different, and I admit I was frightened and completely spooked out. Despite my uncle's gentle reassurance that it was ok, and it was as though Nan was asleep, I felt so scared. But with his comfort and support, I was able to sit with her for a while in her home, just as we had found her.

That day changed my relationship with my dad forever. No-one and nothing could have set us up for what had happened, but it was me that was there for him, and it's a day we will share forever.

The rest of that day I felt numb. When they came to take my nan away, my dad made me sit in her bedroom so that I didn't see her go. He was adamant I wasn't to watch her being taken away from her house. So instead, I sat on her bed, mascara all over my face, while one of my friends comforted me. She had come to go along on our girls' trip, but she was my rock that day.

Going forward, our whole family was broken, and I don't think any of us have ever fully healed. We never will. My dad did so much for my nan, and my parents' married life had been dedicated to being there for her. She was my dad's world and my mum's. After her passing, Mum struggled for so long not having her on the doorstep. The impact of her loss affected us all in so many ways, and we all suffered.

As I was living in Essex, I could drive away from the small pocket of houses I grew up in and all the memories we shared, but my parents still live there, within sight of Nan's house, so it's always been much harder for them.

I am so lucky that with my ability to connect to spirit, I hold her close, and she never lets me down when I need her for extra support with my work, my readings, my shows – and most of all, my life! I can call upon her, obviously not at all hours of the day or when it suits me, but I am able to bring her energy in close. In physical terms, it feels more like a presence.

When she left us, the trauma of that day haunted me for a long time, and I struggled to sleep. Every time I closed my eyes, I could see her lying on that kitchen floor. It scared me shitless, and I would break out in a cold sweat at night, my heart racing, and panic setting in. I was too scared to sleep and was struggling so much, being pregnant with Jasmine that I was taken under the special care department at our local hospital. The midwife there worked closely with me, monitoring me weekly, and I was given regular checks to make sure the baby and I were as healthy as possible.

But I struggled to talk about my nan, what happened, or of my feelings about her passing. I just didn't want to feel the fear I felt, and by fear I mean the haunting.

Chapter Eight

In the early days of my pregnancy, after Nan's passing, I suffered a small bleed and went in for a scan, expecting the worst. I was told that while I had indeed passed a pregnancy, I had kept two! So, Jasmine had initially been a triplet. At the age of 21 and flooded in grief, I was now expecting non-identical twins!

We were pre-warned at that early stage that it was common to lose a twin, something known as 'vanishing twin syndrome' – a miscarriage that causes a pregnancy involving twins to become a pregnancy with just one baby. It occurs when one of the embryos stops developing, generally before the 12th week. We were told there was a 50% chance of this when there were triplets, so I wasn't sure how things would go for us, and I felt as though I was in a brain fog.

At a time when everything should have felt magical, I was shocked to the point that I burst out laughing in the scanning room. I thought it was a joke, and initially nervous laughter kicked in.

I was extremely underweight, and as I was carrying twins, I was told the hospital would keep a closer eye on me. At 10 weeks, we still had two babies and two heartbeats… but unfortunately at 16 weeks, we had two babies and only one heartbeat.

Depression was setting in, and I was exhausted from the sleepless nights of feeling haunted by nans passing.

I had experienced depression before – when I was 18, following the break-up with my first proper boyfriend – and I still believe the depression was a major factor in the crazy credit card spending I did at that time. That break-up was extremely hostile and fully my fault, to be fair, but it still hit me hard. I was put on anti-depressants, and that was my first experience of dealing with my mental health.

I'm sure now that this is why spirit were always trying to stop me from making the stupid choices I did. They knew these choices would hurt me more in the long run, and they always tried to push me away from that hurt.

Now that I use my psychic intuition more, I remember that I would often hear a massive message of 'STOP!' in my ear, or have a 'gut feeling' to make a better choice. Not that I did. It's only now that I can be grateful for those shitty times and the learning I have done, as it means I can finally help others.

There were three times during my early grieving process that my nan came to me when I did manage to sleep.

In one dream we were at a wedding, and we were all sitting around a big table – the usual round tables in a wedding setting – my grandad was there, too. Nan leant across the table and said, 'I know about the baby.' I hadn't told her about the pregnancy before she passed, because it was such early days and, with the uncertainty of the twins, we took a while to share our news. But in the dream, she tapped my hand and said softly, 'I know.'

I was glad she came to me in the dream, but afterwards I would go from uncontrollable crying to feeling angry to feeling terrified. I genuinely thought I was going mad! I would go to bed and lie with the duvet over my head, as I was so scared of what I had seen that day we lost her. Even though she had looked so peaceful, it had still been a horrible shock.

After months of not sleeping properly and being so unsettled, unwell, and struggling through the early days of my pregnancy, my nan came again in another dream. This time, we stood together outside her house, and the sun was shining and the blossom on the trees was blowing everywhere – just as it did on the day of her funeral. (Although it was an October day, the blossom on her tree still remained, and it blew gently before I got in the car to go to her funeral.) I could see so much blossom when I was with her in my dream.

She looked the same as I'd always remembered, wearing the clothes she had always worn, and she told me, 'I can't rest until you do.' It was like that awful day was being wiped out from my life when she added, 'Please rest. I can't until you do.'

So that's what I did, and I started to build my strength back up again.

It wasn't until I had my beautiful baby in my arms that Nan came back to 'visit' me a third time. One night, I woke up and I saw her leaning over Jasmine's baby basket. But I wasn't scared, I knew I wasn't going mad, and I felt so lucky I had Nan by my side. There is that saying 'when one life ends another begins', and I believe my nan saved Jasmine for me.

For years after her passing, I had been unable to bear having any photos of Nan around me. I remember going to visit my oldest sister, Mel, and she had a photo of her up, but I couldn't look at it and had to turn the picture around when I was there. Seeing Nan's face just took me back to that awful day, and the fear, panic, and pain would come flooding back.

The strange thing is, though, I always felt she was watching me. Now, I would use the word 'guiding', but back then it just shit me up, and I was scared of that grief, the black feeling in my heart of finding her dead that day. I was still so angry that it was me that had been there. Why did it have to be me? I was only there because I was going on a girls' weekend, so why did it have to be that day? I was a ball of emotions, and I wanted to know why she died.

She was 88, loved and adored, had such a special family around her, so I couldn't understand why she had to leave us! But a post-mortem wasn't done, and I respect that she would never have wanted that. Nan was fiercely independent, so I feel she chose to go in that way because she would have hated to be so unwell that we needed to care for her. She chose her time, with no suffering, and at her little home, in her kitchen where she spent most of her days. Just how it was supposed to be.

All these years later, I'm now *relieved* that I was there that day, and I'm glad it was me that looked after my dad. I know it was all part of her plan – the longer plan to give strength to my relationship with Dad. Losing her affected my life, and although no-one might have noticed it straight away, it changed me forever.

Being scared of spirit seems crazy now when I think about what I do when I connect to them. Being a medium, I speak to clients all over the world and connect to strangers – passed-away loved ones that I don't even know. So you would think that would be scarier than my nan, who I grew up with and had such a close relationship with.

I can understand now that she was helping me to move forward from the trauma. It was only the physical body of her lying on her kitchen floor, but her spirit and kind soul had already left. She was already doing her work from the other side in spirit world just by coming to me in my dreams as early on as she did, and by the way I relayed to my dad that she was with grandad already.

Dreaming is the easiest way for spirit to come to you, because your mind is at rest, open and ready to allow messages in. From a young age I knew I had it – 'it' being what most people call the 'gift'. That is a term I choose not to use, because in my eyes the gift is from spirit, not from me. The gift they give to me is the message, the clarity, and the detail they provide when they come to me for the client. *I* don't have the gift; it's who I am. So, I'm being me each time I connect and give someone a message.

Chapter Nine

Thinking back, I was eight years old when I experienced 'it' for the first time. My dad's aunt lived directly next door to our semi-detached house. She was my nan's sister, such a soft natured lady, Auntie Nancy.

Growing up, I was always in and out of her house, just sitting chatting with her. But towards the end of her life, she became very unwell with Motor Neurone Disease and lost the ability to talk. Knowing what I know now about MND, I wonder how on earth I didn't notice how unwell she had become. She always looked the same to me, but her spirit had already left her physical body, and what was left of her on earth wasn't really her – it was just the shell of her physical body left. So, I was in fact talking to her spirit the whole time.

Lying in my bed in the weeks after her passing, I always felt her presence. But I wasn't scared, and nor did I do the hiding-under-the-duvet thing I found myself doing all those years later when I was an adult. I liked Auntie Nancy's kindness and soft nature, but her personality still lingered around me as a feeling for months after.

My dad's sister had been my confidante and friend from my early childhood, so I was encouraged to tell her about my feelings. She is also a medium, and she taught me to wrap myself up symbolically in a big, blue fluffy blanket. This is a technique I now offer a lot to help others protect themselves and their children if they feel spirit have come to visit them.

Children's minds are open and clear of environmental influences of other thoughts. Spirit doesn't come to scare or cause harm; it just means they have seen a way in, so they take the way back to earth and run with it. I describe it as 'if the light is on, someone is home'.

From that young age, I just got into the habit of wrapping myself in the blue blanket every night. It became normal for me to do that to quieten the 'noise' in my mind that I can only describe as sounding like a packed dinner hall. This gave me the protection every night to close my mind down and just make spirit aware that I wasn't ready for this... yet.

I was fascinated by my auntie. She was the only one who understood me when it came to talking about spirit, and she would take me along to spiritual church meetings. When you think of a church, you think of a big, grand building and lots of religious stuff going on, but it wasn't like that at all. It was a place where you could go and sit, listen, and watch other mediums take to the front and connect to spirit. If you knew that the person coming through the medium was speaking directly to you, you took the message. Between the ages of about 12 and 17, I was visiting these churches on and off, but I only ever got one message in all that time.

The message was from my grandad (Nan's husband), who had passed away when I was 11. I often wonder how my nan felt having to carry on life without him all those years, until her day came to make the path back to him.

A few days before the message at church, I had been coming down the stairs at home, aged 14, when I felt someone touch my ear. It was the back of my right ear, like a flick.

Later that week, my aunt and I attended one of the meetings which included some of the regular mediums – an elderly husband and wife duo that I liked. It was the man who picked me out, and he spoke about my grandad. I could relate to most of the detail he gave, but as soon as he mentioned the touch to the ear, I knew.

I've come to realise that no matter how much you can describe someone to confirm who they are, there is always one moment in a reading when the client gets their confirmation.

It can be something so small but so meaningful to them, and the light bulb goes off and they know you have their loved one. I now know this is a priceless offering for people.

If I'm reading online, what my clients don't see is the happy dance I do when this lightbulb moment happens, or when a client leaves the room and I'm fist-pumping the air like a lunatic, high-fiving their spirit relatives who gave me that moment!

The drive to and from those church meetings always gave me a chance to ask my aunt a million questions, and I found the whole subject so fascinating. But that was as far as my relationship with mediumship went at that stage in my life. I was off to join the Army (remember?). And when that didn't come to fruition, I was going to conquer the beauty industry.

Life had other plans, though; it was a never-ending roller-coaster.

Chapter Ten

Believe me that when I say being the 'third person' in my relationship with Mr R had never been a life goal, but neither was becoming a struggling single mum.

Let me take you back to 2013.

Alone, tirelessly packing up the boxes of my house, preparing my kids to move for the second time since leaving their father two years before. After so long trying to pluck up the courage to walk from a controlling relationship, I had finally taken my six-year-old daughter and my four-month-old baby boy to live in a place of our own. I hoped it would be somewhere I could maybe find some peace and solitude from the volatile relationship I had spent so long in, somewhere I could find my voice again, discover who I was and who I wanted to become. For so long I had just existed through the days and then the sleepless nights, arguing till the early hours, having someone talk at me and telling me who I should and shouldn't be, what I could and couldn't do – mostly couldn't, if I'm honest.

I always remember he really enjoyed telling me what I couldn't do and reminding me of what I wasn't doing right. From the moment I had my daughter, I had just wanted to be the best mum I could be, and knowing that he assumed I would fail, I guess I became even more obsessed about being the ultimate mother.

I wanted to prove him wrong, but after so long being degraded and criticised time and time again, you eventually start to believe what someone tells you.

I didn't even bother trying to explain that I was a good person. I just wanted peace. I wanted love and a family of my own.

Our relationship wasn't always bad, and I often think that in another life we might have been perfect for each other. Maybe it would have been easier if I had been older. I was still so young when we met, but I loved him so much.

I'm sure *he* would still say to this day that it was me who caused the breakdown, that I wasn't enough, and he could recite a whole list of wrongdoings by me. But this was my life, and it wasn't going the way it was supposed to.

We had two beautiful children – first a girl, then a boy. My God, how lucky were we! But something always ruined a lovely day. The sun could be shining, and we could be spending a day together with the children, but he would still have to drink no matter what time of day it was.

He was always the life and soul of every room, but when we got home, everything changed. I dreaded it. I would literally be sweating all the way home, begging the universe to just get us indoors, settle the kids, and him fall asleep on the sofa. When he did, I would creep about not to wake him, but it got to a point where I felt deeply unhappy and so sad, lost, and broken.

On the bad days, or the day after the bad nights, I would make sure I was out before he woke up. I would just pack a lunch for Jasmine (before Reggie was born) and find somewhere nice to sit in my car with her. It was peaceful and calm, and that's all I needed most of the time.

I was losing who I was, and as far as my daughter was concerned, that just wasn't an option. Then my little boy came along, and all through the nights of my ex being drunk, aggressive, and abusive, all I could think was that I did not want my son to be that type of man nor my daughter to be with a man like him. It was my responsibility to just try and do the right thing for them.

It's mad how you can love someone so much but just feel so lost around them, to a point where I didn't even know why or how the love was still there. I still loved him, and I would always think back to better times to try and seek strength and remind myself that our relationship wasn't all bad. I carried a photo of him around with me from that holiday he had surprised me with for my 21st birthday, pre-children. On the back of the photo, I had written 'I forgive you', because I did. I always did. But the constant anxiety saw me back on antidepressants again, and my mental health was in need of attention.

I remember going to the GP after I had my daughter and asking him if he would take my baby away if I went on antidepressants. He was mortified that I would even consider something like that. Getting the help that I needed was the best thing I could do for my baby, he told me, and he reassured me that I was going to be ok and I was an amazing mum. He knew it wasn't me that was the problem, as he had witnessed the kids' dad's controlling ways when he'd come along to check-up appointments and would do all the talking for me.

Now I can see how confused and mixed-up my thinking was then. My doctor would look at me with such sad eyes when I went to him for help, because I begged him multiple times not to give me medication in case I lost my children. He knew I had been brainwashed into believing this, but at the time the fog was growing thicker in my mind and clarity was becoming lost. The GP was also aware that my relationship was volatile, as I had on a previous occasion been to see him for the human bite on my arm that resulted in me being administered antibiotics.

People often say they have a good doctor, and I was definitely fortunate in that respect. He never once pushed me to share information I didn't want to talk about, and he kept reassuring me that I hadn't lost my mind and that I wouldn't lose my children just because I was asking for help with my mental health. He would always say, 'You're a clever girl, Amy. Don't ever give up, you can be anything!'

I used to come out of his appointments smiling, reminded of my hopes and dreams, and the fog always seemed a little clearer each time I left. He played a massive role in saving me, and I was so grateful to him for continually reminding me of my worth.

I was never honest with my ex about my medication. He had convinced me that if I was ill, I would lose the kids. And if I left him, he threatened to take them from me because I wasn't 'well enough' to be a good mum to them. These threats and the constant criticism started in the early days after I'd had Jasmine and continued until after Reggie was born. Many times, in alcohol-fuelled confrontation, he would tell me that he would prove I was mental and not stable enough to look after them.

Now, I can clearly see how absolutely ludicrous his threats were, but I was terrified at the time, and I felt he had all the power and control. Everything I did revolved around my kids, and being the best mum to them had become a total obsession which was verging on unhealthy.

By the time I left their dad, the kids were all I had. I wasn't successful. I was struggling for money badly – actually, struggling wasn't the case; I had none! Anything I earned had always had to be accounted for, and he had kept an eye on anything I spent – another form of control. Heaven forbid I might want to treat myself to anything!

On numerous occasions I reached out to my ex's mother to ask for help with his unhealthy addictions. On one occasion, I when she came to visit, I was sitting on the floor with my six-day old son in my arms. Yet again the red wine was flowing by lunchtime, but still no-one said anything. At one point he asked me what my intentions were for work. Our daughter was five years old at this point, ready to start big school, and my little baby boy wasn't even one week old, but he announced bluntly, 'Don't think you're going to sponge off me. You need to get off your arse and work.'

My mind went into a blind panic, and all I could think about at that point was how I was going to juggle everything with no childcare. He wouldn't look after the kids to allow me to work, so I'd had to do early morning office cleaning jobs, starting at 5am while Jasmine was asleep, and coming home at 7am to wake her and start our day. I'd done that right up until my pregnancy with Reggie, but hadn't planned to continue after he was born. Was this all my life was going to be?

When I first met my ex, I still lived with my parents and had no idea how to run a household. Not only did I have no idea about the financial burden of it, but I couldn't even fry an egg when I moved in with him. One thing he did teach me was to cook, but then I realised it was because he liked everything his way, from the way his burgers were flipped to the way his sandwiches were cut.

So, 2013, there I was packing boxes again for the second time since leaving him, and I still didn't have a pot to piss in. I lost the first house the kids and I moved into because I literally could not afford it: if I paid my rent, I couldn't pay bills; if I paid bills, we couldn't eat. It was a never-ending shit show. But not once did I ever regret leaving him!

The family house was his property. I always felt that me and the kids just lived there, and it never felt like a real home. But when I moved out with the kids into rented accommodation, it was such a financial struggle that I felt like a total let-down. The night before the monthly rent was due, I would feel sick knowing the money wasn't there to pay. I was getting some government support, but there was a huge deficit between what people think of 'single mum help' and how much you have to actually pay out to live. Even living in a one bed flat, the deficit was massive. I was fucked all the time, and that's before bills and food and petrol!

I had been fully aware when I took on the tenancies that it was going to be a struggle, yet I felt that somehow I would manage to make it work. Surely it wasn't that hard to run a house? But financially I was sinking. In fact, I had well and truly sunk.

When the second tenancy went wrong, I packed every single box of that house up on my own and dragged every single one out to the back garden ready for the removal van to come. It had been sent to me and paid for, and I felt like such a charity case.

I had no deposit to move anywhere else, and my car was a £75 banger from a car auction and literally ran on thin air. My friends all knew that I would run out of fuel all the time. My friendship with one of my best friends, Kerry, started when she saved my arse from another breakdown with no fuel. She went from being a lovely school mum who kindly helped me get my car started again that day, to being one of the biggest supports in my life. I wish I had known then that with every negative comes a positive.

I kept thinking that all I needed my car for was to make sure my daughter could get to school, but I broke down due to no fuel more times than I made it. The choice between fuel or food was always a tricky one, but I made sure the kids always had good dinners and they always looked clean and tidy to other people. From the outside looking in, I know I looked like I had all my shit together, but I can't count the amount of times I used my car as a haven or therapy room, crying, screaming in that pile of tin, begging the universe to give me a break, an opening to just something better, at least something that would mean I could give the kids dessert! There were so many times I stood in the supermarket unloading my shopping before going through the checkout, dreading the bill and wondering if I'd added it all up in my head properly, working out what would have to be put back on the shelf, sick at the thought of being even one pound over – because I just didn't have that extra pound.

Cakes, treats, and desserts weren't a thing in our household for such a long time, but my kids weren't deprived. I simply had to make choices, and making a meal last for two days was more important than buying a pot of ice cream.

It's funny, but both my kids now hate shepherd's pie. It was my go-to hearty meal in those times, because we could have it again the next day and it was cheap to make. Now they can't even stand the smell of it, and the ongoing joke is, 'We're not having shepherd's pie again, are we, Mum?' The comment makes me smile, but it's a reminder that I have to keep working hard and keep my visions bigger.

During this time of penny-pinching, robbing Peter to pay Paul, I still had my phone ringing at all hours with drunken calls and relentless verbal abuse, calling me 'useless, mental, a liar, a slag'. So late nights, worry, and sadness became normal life for me. One of my friends who lived nearby, Jenny, always knew when I'd had a bad night. She would see me on the school run in the mornings, take one look, and just knew. She had me and the kids over for dinner so many times – I would say four nights out of the seven – and she became my family. Her husband never made me feel a burden, and she was a saviour feeding us, whilst my children thought they were on a constant playdate.

At home, I didn't really eat much unless my dad came over and took me to the supermarket to fill up a huge trolley. They were my best moments: full trolley, full fridge – one massive problem solved for a few weeks. My mum and dad supported me the best they could, but they didn't have lots of money. My dad has ill health and was medically retired while me, my three sisters, and my niece were growing up, and Mum cares for him. It's now that I appreciate them even more, particularly when I realise that there was always food on the table when we were growing up, and not once did my parents share their fears about finances.

When Jasmine and Reggie were asleep, I'd lie awake all night dreading the fact I had to get up the next day and attempt the daily norm of running the household with fresh air, trying to push what little bit of income I had coming in to the max and beyond. I did nails and eyebrows for some clients, which I loved because it gave me a feeling that I was actually something. But in my head I always had big plans, big dreams, and I just wanted to have the kids set up with a stable life. The biggest dream of that time was being able to know my home was safe and that the kids wouldn't have to move again.

In case you're wondering where the kids' dad was with financial support during this time – there wasn't any. I could have begged him to help, and I'm sure I did before having to pack up this second house. But money was another form of control for him, and I'm certain he assumed I would go back to him if I was on my arse without options. If I'm honest, there were many, many times I felt like I should go back, and I questioned whether I should have just shut up, put up, and stayed with him until the kids were older. You hear people say all the time that they're unhappy then add, 'I'll see how I feel when the kids are older.' But I just couldn't do it. The pain I felt in my heart all the time, and the sickening feeling of fear about what the next day would bring, meant I just had to get out.

There was little support available from official organisations then either, although I didn't expect handouts and never expected to not pay my way. As far as I was concerned, this was always a temporary measure to get back on my feet whilst my children were so young.

I went to the government office daily and was given a case worker because I was going to be homeless. I coughed my way through meetings with constant chest infections, feeling so unwell I was pretty much on the floor, and with little Reggie in his pram. The case worker would often look at me and just stop, tilt her head, and say, 'Are you ok?' I wanted to scream back, 'DO I LOOK OK?!'

For weeks prior to packing up that second house and getting ready to leave, I begged for a one-bedroom flat to get us housed. But her reply was, 'Your ex, the children's father, has a duty of care to house his children until they are 16. You left his property and made yourself homeless.' Despite the fact that she knew I had left a volatile relationship, and had my doctor's and police records to prove it, her answer was, 'You could go back and sleep in a different room and work out a rota for the shared rooms.'

I had no words.

Now, though, I would like to say thank you to that official organisation who showed me no care. They simply saw me as a number, and maybe as another freeloader. But as it turns out, they played an important part in my journey.

I remember begging my mum one night on the phone to please let me come home. But she knew it wasn't what I really wanted and I wouldn't have been happy. Nor did I want to take Jasmine out of her school where I'd been shown so much support and made friends who had become my family.

I'd moved to Essex at the age of 20, after I met the kids' dad and fell in love. It was a bold move to leave behind my job, my friends, and my parents, but I managed to build some kind of life. And it wasn't always bad…

Truthfully, I didn't want to move back to Bedfordshire, but somehow this pain had to go. My mental health was declining, and when the kids were settled in bed, I felt so alone. Leaving someone is tough; leaving someone you love is tougher; and remembering the reasons why is painful. Being with the kids' dad was all I had known for such a long time, and he had been a huge part of my life.

I used to lie beside my daughter for hours at bedtime. She was my safe place – something that started when we lived with their dad. When he was going off on one, drunk and completely irrational, verbally abusing me, I would go and lie beside her, as I knew he wouldn't come into her room and disturb her. It was the only time and place where I felt safe.

My kids have always been my safe place; the place I truly know as 'home'.

But now I was packing up boxes again, with nowhere to go, i found myself sitting in my car crying and just praying something would change

Chapter Eleven

The universe finally heard my cries.

A nail client who had become a friend of mine heard about my plight and reached out to an ex-employer of hers. He had a transport business where he also had static caravans to rent, and she was sure he would find a way to help me, fully aware I had no money, no deposit, two amazing young kids, and an unruly out-of-control ex who used to create havoc at all hours on my doorstep. And help is what he did.

The potential landlord arranged a meeting at my house. I was in the last few days of my tenancy, so this was the last chance saloon, and he was coming to discuss what he had to offer and my options. On the way to my house that evening, he called and asked if I needed anything, arriving with milk, coffee, and a fizzy drink. Clearly, I was not the hostess with the mostest! He wanted coffee, and as I don't like hot drinks, he had to provide it himself.

As I was a little on edge about the meeting, I had asked Jenny to come over and play chaperone. But Sod's law, just as he came through the door, I got a text from her that she couldn't make it. Damn, I'd need to do this alone!

He made me feel really uneasy, but not in a threatening way. It was just that he was everything I wasn't – powerful and wealthy, judging by the success of his business. He had an aura about him, to the point that I sat on the opposite end of the sofa as I just couldn't be too close to him.

We spoke briefly about a caravan that he offered me to live in, and he showed me some photos of it on his phone. And that was how the universe gave me my big break; I just didn't know it then.

My guard was still up, though, and I couldn't wait for the potential landlord – all smooth and cool, tall, dark, and handsome – to get out of my house. But he had offered us a real chance, and I decided to take it.

I grew up spending many summers in a caravan with my family and I'd loved it, but this was different. It hurt my heart that I was going to move my kids out of a beautiful three-bedroom house in a lovely Essex housing estate to live in a mobile home on a transport yard, with articulated lorries outside my front room window! A transport yard and storage container depot, which proved to be boiling hot and dusty in the summer and soaking wet, muddy, and freezing in the winter.

I was just six months off my 30th birthday, and being in this situation had never been the plan! I had always wanted to be married by the time I was 30, as it felt like such a big grown-up number, and I wanted to be successful in my own right. I remember a conversation with my other nan (my mum's mum). I always told her I would be famous one day, and she would always agree with me. I must have been about ten when I said it again one day, and she said in her Scottish accent, 'I don't doubt it, darling. What are you going to be famous for?'

My reply was, 'Being me!' Ha, ha.

But she always believed that I could. I would see it in her eyes. She and I would come up with crazy ideas on long journeys up north where she lived, talking about how we would set up a business or ways to make me famous. Yet now I felt like I had come to nothing in my life. The same month I moved into the caravan, my best friend, Vicki, bought her first house. I was living in a different world to my friends, and I don't think they even knew how bad it was at times. But you have to live it to know it. I'm sure so many of my friends hold some sort of guilt around what I went through, but they have no need to. They all played their part in rebuilding me, which I have never forgotten, and my gratitude to them runs deeper than any ocean.

In my eyes, Amy wasn't anything important, other than Mummy. Little did I know that when you *think* you're nothing, that is exactly what you become. However, I grew to learn that *thoughts* become *things*.

I don't even remember how I told the kids we were moving again. I just know I shut the door on the house and returned the key to the agent. I was in my tracksuit, with scraped-back hair, my body was worn out, my skin was a mess, and my bank balance was well in the minus – only the debts were in the plus. I was done in, but I was so relieved to shut the door on that house. When the place you live becomes a burden, it's no longer a 'home'.

Again, my parents helped me move. They loved the caravan as soon as they saw it, but I know they just saw what was right for me at that time. The added bonus, though, was that I was too far away in the next town for my ex to turn up drunk and cause havoc, and the yard was set in private land.

On the other hand, no-one knew how to get there. It was so hidden away, down a long, dirt track, that my parcels got lost and my pizza was never delivered on time. But it was like living in another world.

My neighbours were all lorry drivers or people that worked in the yard, and initially I felt totally out of my depth, but at the same time I felt free. Reggie was in his element – lorries, a working yard of men, and so many good people to look after us and take us under their wing. And that's exactly what they did. For the first time in a long time, I felt like I actually belonged somewhere and I had people looking out for me. I was so safe and secure.

My landlord didn't pressure me for a deposit or rent at that stage, but allowed me time to just settle. He knew this caravan was my lifeline. My parents thought he was wonderful, of course, because he had given me this whole new life and they felt they didn't have to worry about me so much. They knew I had people looking after me, especially my landlord.

In my own mind, I imagined I would get my shit together, build up more clients and get some money to move out. I kept telling myself, and the kids, that it was 'temporary'. I'd say, 'Don't worry, kids, when we get a house…' with every sentence. When we get a house, we can do this. When we get a house, we can have that.

The view from the front room window of our new home was of lorries, cars, portable offices, and storage containers – one of which was mine, and where I stored my life. I had my wardrobes in there, so I often ran across the yard in my dressing gown to get my clothes.

I had a thought once that maybe I could turn my storage container into a little salon. God knows how I would do it, but in my mind, I had this big idea that I could divide it into two: my storage on one side, all hidden; and a little salon on the other side.

My visions were always big. It was being able to make my plans a reality that was the problem, as I couldn't ever get past the thought stage. My brain was full of ideas but with no way of making them come to fruition. I just didn't know how.

I've come to learn that the HOW didn't matter. All I had to do was trust that I would get to the destination.

My children had their own rooms in the caravan, which I was so grateful for, and it was much more than lots of other children had. But by the time we moved in, the stress had taken its toll on me, and I started to be sick most nights, which resulted in a stomach ulcer that I suffered for over a year.

That first year of living there I was constantly unwell. I lost weight and I suffered numerous chest infections. One morning, I woke up from a night of coughing to find cough medicine on my doorstep. Wow! This was my new life where people had my back. I was choking my guts up from such a bad cough, but at least I was in my little heaven of freedom.

Chapter Twelve

During the first few months of my new life at the yard, my landlord couldn't have done more for me. He really made us feel welcome, made my caravan so lovely, and helped with absolutely anything I needed. But I still felt there was still something very intimidating about him.

I was starting to wonder if he fancied me. But why would he? I didn't have anything to offer him. I knew he had a wife and a family of his own, so I told myself I was reading it all wrong.

He did compliment me a lot And he was genuinely interested in me; he listened to me when I spoke.

Losing so much confidence with the kids' dad, I rarely looked up when I spoke to people, and I often wore sunglasses. But the landlord would ask to see my eyes when I was speaking to him.

He was keen to hear about my plans, hopes, and visions, and what I really wanted from my life. Even from those early months, I could see that he believed in me, but this wasn't how a platonic relationship would usually go with your landlord, was it? Was I missing something? He always had time for my children, too. They were quickly building a friendly relationship of their own with him, at seven and two, and they had created a circle of trust with him. My kids weren't stupid, and they could see how much I was changing thanks to this opportunity. Maybe it was me that had to do the same.

Yet I just wasn't in any way ready to be involved with anyone, and I wanted to protect my children at all costs. I hadn't dated much since leaving their dad, as I still loved him for such a long time, and I was still grieving the loss of our relationship.

There was only one guy that I spent proper time with, and he was what I now call 'the middle man'. He taught me that I was finally ready to move on, to let go and be ok with the fact that I was never going back to the kids' dad, it was over, and that part of my life was finished.

And he was right. I'll never take away from my ex that he *is* their dad, and I will always love him for that, but our relationship was well and truly over. I had no energy for it, particularly not the rowing – and there was a hell of a lot more of that to come. It took me three years after leaving him to realise that it was over, and the middle man played a vital role in that.

My health and getting my shit together were the most important things now. I also initially felt quite embarrassed that I was having to live in a caravan, so being with someone romantically wasn't right for me. I had lost faith and trust in almost everything.

But my new landlord changed that for me. I knew from the friend who had introduced us that he was a genuinely good and kind person, but I didn't know what was happening between us. He would make excuses to be alone with me, or help me load my storage and then accidentally hold my hand or brush past me. He let me drive one of the artic lorries into a parking bay in the yard, which was fun, but of course he had to be the one to help me drive it!

He started to make it obvious to me what he wanted, and I saw clearly that it was me! Somehow, I needed to keep the situation at arm's length. I didn't want anyone to think I was just some single mum with no money, sleeping her way to paying her rent. That wasn't me at all, and I wanted people in the yard to get to know me for who I really was and respect me for the fact I was aiming to get my life back together.

Hooking up with the landlord, or starting any sort of relationship with him, just wasn't a good look – besides the fact that he was married. When he tried to flirt with me, I found myself telling him it would open a whole can of worms. I don't even know what I meant at the time; I just knew if something started between us, it wouldn't stop...

I mentioned earlier the devastation of my nan passing away and how it affected me for such a long time. I had never been to visit her grave in the ten years since she had passed, as she had always told us not to go there. She said she wasn't in a cemetery, but would always be with us – and she was bloody well right. The only place I would go to feel closer to her was a bench on a Norfolk cliff – a place where we spent all our childhood holidays, where both Nan and Grandad would stand with us looking out to sea. They both loved it there, so the bench was my happy place to be with Nan.

She was such a spiritual lady, although I never noticed it when she was alive as much as I should have. She spent all those days still chatting to my grandad after his passing, and I should have known then how spiritual she was.

The main reason I didn't go to visit her grave, though, was because I was scared of the pain it would bring. When I told my landlord the story of her passing, and that I had been dealing with her death the best I could for ten years, he encouraged me to go. He offered to take me there, and I'm so glad he did.

During the 60-mile car journey to my nan's resting place, we chatted about the loss of his mother, but he was unemotional and detached talking about her. He had lost her at a young age and didn't believe there was anything after death, but I felt her around me when he spoke about her.

I wasn't a practising medium at that time in my life. I was still pursuing the world of eyebrows and nails, but I felt her presence in the same way I had felt my dad's aunt all those years before. I could sense his mother's personality, the way she looked, and the way she sounded, all in my mind's eye.

I trusted that presence was a positive sign and it meant she also approved of me and my growing relationship with her son.

Her strength and kind heart are qualities he has inherited, and I appreciated her presence in that moment, just as I would for many years to follow.

When we eventually arrived at Milton Keynes cemetery, I knew it was time. I had suppressed the pain of Nan's death for ten long years, but there was nowhere for the emotions to hide now.

26th January, 2016, Milton Keynes cemetery

When we drove through the cemetery gates, it looked exactly the same as I remembered. It was as though nothing had changed, but at the same time everything was different. It had been ten long years since I'd been here for her funeral, and I had been so scared to go back, fearful that the gut-wrenching pain of losing her would come back into my heart again as raw as it had in the past.

I was never my nan's favourite grandchild – not that she would admit it, ha, ha! There were so many of us, but since her passing I felt closer to her than ever before. Even from the spirit world she could see I was struggling and that life hadn't always been kind to me. She clearly knew this would always be the case as once on a family holiday, when I was about 15, she told me, 'Nothing in your life will come easily.'

Those words. What an odd thing to say. But now, more than ever, she was bloody right.

I couldn't stop crying as I sat on the cemetery ground in the pouring rain. It was cold and dark, and I could smell the dampness in the air. I was there for hours, but it felt like minutes, begging her to tell me how to move forward with my life, to give me direction and, above everything, some hope. People that know me would say that I'm a strong character, but in that moment, I felt like a vulnerable child.

I felt so lost and afraid. I needed to know what to do and where my future would lead. In my head, I repeated over and over, *Please, Nan, please can you help me?*

Then the rain stopped, and clear as day I heard her voice tell me, 'Turn around.'

I did as she told me and, standing with his hand reaching out to me, was my landlord... Mr R.

I knew what I had to do.

Chapter Thirteen

October 2015.

Moving to the caravan was an adventure; the kids were over the moon with their bedrooms, and it was like a permanent holiday. Thankfully, they had no idea how I was feeling inside.

I had sliding doors in my lounge/kitchen area, so I could open them wide in the summertime when the caravan was so hot you couldn't breathe. But it was that greenhouse effect, so in the winter if it snowed or went below freezing, the water froze over, and I had to buy bottled water – the massive gallon bottles – to brush our teeth and wash with. It was so cold on one particular snowy night that the three of us slept in my bed to keep warm.

I could see in the kids' eyes that they weren't scared of anything when I was around. They would look at me for reassurance and I always gave it to them, even if I was crying inside or losing hope in what options I had. They always had the reassurance that they were loved, safe, and that I was always going to be there for them.

In the early days of living in the caravan, I found it hard not to be embarrassed when people asked the kids or me about where we lived. I was worried that people would think I had put my kids' needs last by leaving their dad, taking them from a lovely home with him but then being unable to provide a roof over their heads and ending up in a caravan. I could almost hear them saying, 'Why would she do that? Amy is a let-down again.' All the insults their dad used to say to me were embedded in my brain.

I often wondered if he was laughing at me, watching me fail. But the truth is, the caravan wasn't a failure! That little haven we called home saved me.

When we moved in, I unloaded all my life and all our stuff into one of the storage containers, so that I could get the essentials sorted first and then take out slowly what I needed. Downsizing from a three-bedroom house to a caravan really opens your eyes to what's important and what's really needed, and how to utilise space became key to comfortable living.

Reggie was always just running around, and his love for the outdoors was fulfilled in our new home. The smell of the yard was of lorry fuel, dust, and earth, but I loved the smell of the earth and the view of the clear starry sky at night. It was so silent you could hear a pin drop – totally different from the functioning busy yard of the daytime.

It was so peaceful, and the sound of silence became the only way I could try and keep the visions or the use of my imagination alive in my mind. As I said before, I had a plan of six months to get myself sorted, more clients maybe, and more established in a business that would sustain a lifestyle of security of some kind and put me in a position to get a house again.

I would look at Vicki, who was buying her house at that time, and imagine being a bit like her. She had a successful career, could do huge food shops, always had lovely clothes, and was always the first to suggest a night out. She has an absolute heart of gold, and I was always so happy for her successes. We had become friends when I rented a space in a shop doing nails (Laura's shop) not long after I had Jasmine. On a Saturday I would do a full day there, as my mum would come and stay to take care of Jasmine, and Vicki had her business next door. Eventually (along with Laura and her sister-in-law Mandy) they became what I labelled my 'Table for Four' girls.

Vicki's mum, Kim, was a powerful businesswoman and everything I aspire to be. Even the way she walked was infectious. I used to pine for her contact just so I could soak up her strong business ways. It was an addiction, and still is. Kim always looked like a successful businesswoman, by her clothes, the way she spoke, and her mannerisms, and you knew straight away that she had her shit together and loads of success under her belt. So, it was only natural that Vicki would follow in her footsteps. I was constantly inspired by them both, and I desperately wanted a business, success, and to build something where my kids could say proudly, 'That's my mum.' But it was so tough when my reality was a million miles away from theirs.

A few weeks into living in the caravan, I started to make it nice so that the kids' bedrooms were lovely and cosy and they had all the things they loved. I even managed to get Jasmine's desk into her room. She had a passion for playing schools, so she loved her desk. Her room had a built-in dressing table, and she loved sitting there doing her hair. It made her feel so grown up.

My little girl was growing up so fast, but she rarely left my side; she was like glue, and still is. I still lay down with her every night. Reggie, on the other hand, didn't need a thing. He had the outdoors and love of the lorries, the working yard, and the interaction of strong men around him.

I know I keep saying it, but they were so happy. I had some cheap zip-up wardrobes put up in the storage unit to store my clothes, because I only had limited space in my caravan wardrobe, and I would run over to the unit in my dressing gown if I needed anything. As space was limited, the kids also had to alternate their toys. If the doll's pram was indoors, the karaoke machine was out! Ha, ha!

The best thing for me was that, after visiting her grave, I finally had my nan's photo in my living room. I sensed it was right, and I felt at peace that she was guiding me. Knowing I had her there comforted me and I grew strength from her.

Even now when I mention that we lived in a caravan, people are fascinated and have so many questions. I always have to explain that it wasn't a caravan that hooked on the back of the car; it was a three-bed static caravan, but not a flash luxury 'lodge'. It was the kind of caravan you would get on a holiday resort, but without the cool attractions of mini golf, an indoor pool, or a clubhouse. On the edges of the yard were shipping containers, and there was certainly no sea view!

This was no holiday camp; it was our real life.

You had to drive up a long lane, over uneven potholes where the lorries had damaged the road, and through traveller sites on either side. The travellers would no doubt have intimidated many people, but I never felt that at all, and they would always wave as I passed.

Mr R was extremely well respected, and if you were in his yard it was as though you were in a special club. I was the only girl in the yard for ages.

I was teaching my daughter not to let anything we had been through define her. My biggest pet hate is hearing people say, 'Oh well, her parents are separated,' or 'Oh, she lives in a caravan.' Never have my children allowed anything we went through to define them, nor have we used it as an excuse.

And now, all these years later, I'm that girl from the caravan and I'm so bloody proud of it! I'm owning it.

I am that girl.

Chapter Fourteen

We settled in quickly to our new surroundings and way of life, but I was still struggling financially. I was trying to do nails and eyebrows whenever I could, but my income still didn't even meet our basic needs.

I remember a time when it was another of the Table for Four's 30th birthday meal and drinks. I was skint, but I still felt it was so important that I went along. I put £10 petrol in the car to get me there and back, and my mum sent £10 to my bank so that I could have something to eat and to drink water. I had to have everything planned out before I did anything. If I had it planned in my head, then I knew how I would deal with paying for the evening, and that's what I did. I went along to show my love to my friend and we had a lovely time, but it took every last penny. My mum didn't want me missing out, but I was so drained with it all.

I became unwell over these first few weeks and months, with pains in my tummy all the time. I couldn't eat even when I wanted to, as the pain in my belly and the burning in my chest just got worse with food. At times, I'd double over with the pain, then during the night I would wake up around 1am and start throwing up. This went on for months.. My belly was bleeding on the inside from the stomach ulcer, and it felt as though my tummy was on fire, but it was all stress related.

I was in agony, and I lost two stones; on my 30th birthday I was the lightest I've ever been. When I kept saying to people that I couldn't eat, I'm sure they didn't believe me. But I genuinely couldn't eat due to the pain.

When I finally got the treatment and medication I needed, and I started to become well again, the sickness stopped and I could start to heal. Being with my kids is all I need; it's all I'll ever need.

Mr R fussed over me and worried about me. He always went beyond to help us settle in, and I'll never forget the day he made a pallet balcony for my caravan and covered it in artificial grass. It looked so posh in my eyes! It really helped the kids have somewhere they could play rather than in the working yard. Finally, I had privacy, and this was our *home*!

The first time any of my friends would come and visit us at the caravan, I could see they almost wanted to say – and sometimes did – 'I'm sorry' or 'You ok?' in a pitying voice. You know what I mean. Not by being horrible or meaning to be patronising, but some didn't know whether they should be pleased for a mate who had lost everything to go and live in a caravan. It was difficult for some to get it, but they didn't have to. I had a home – one that wouldn't get taken from me, and which gave me a chance to breathe.

Many Friday nights, when my neighbours were home from their week of lorry driving, we would all sit on my artificial grass balcony with a glass of Pimm's and eat a carryout from the chip shop.

I don't think any of them know how much they touched my heart, how much they made my life better, and how grateful I am to them all for loving me and the kids for all we had and all that we were. I didn't even lock my van up most days – only at night (if I remembered) – because it was so safe there and Mr R wasn't too far away. His office was situated in the yard, and the bond he built with people earned their loyalty. It is something I noticed straight away.

You might be wondering how my relationship with Mr R developed from professional to something more. Well… in a nutshell, he made it clear how he felt about me, and all the fuss and the kindness he showed was more than just helping me in my time of need. Some may think he exploited the fact I needed someone to help me, and along comes a knight in shining armour and sweeps me off my feet, gives me a caravan, and makes life as easy as possible... But it was no fairy-tale story.

I don't believe even to this day that his intention was to fall in love with me. And no way did I envisage leaving one bad situation with the kids' dad and moving into a complicated relationship with a married man. He would ask me questions about how I felt about him, which threw me completely. I never knew what to reply, to be honest. I was uncomfortable because I knew he was married. This unsettled me a lot, and I didn't want to be caught in that, nor did it sit right with me.

Truth is, I didn't fancy him at all. He intimidated me a little with his success and his luxury cars, but he wasn't flash, and he had a humble approach to life. You could tell from his attitude to the business that he had worked so hard, and again this was inspiring for me.

And I don't think I've ever met anyone as kind. He was so natural with my children, and would always make comments about how amazing they were, well behaved, polite, and humble. He regularly praised me for their upbringing, and I think he found me inspiring in my own way with the ability to be a single mum.

At the top of the yard there was a skip where we could put our rubbish in the evening. I always enjoyed that time of the day, taking a slow walk up to chuck the rubbish in, enjoying the peace and quiet around me. On one occasion, I was really upset about something, but noticed that someone had had a clear-out and left a load of china plates to be thrown into the skip. I took great pleasure in smashing every single one of them into the skip, literally picking them up one by one, smash, smash, smash! I was in the middle of nowhere in that yard, so my antics didn't bother anyone, and it was soooo good for my mental health!

One evening, I went up as usual to the skip to drop in my rubbish and was joined by Mr R, who was working late. Not romantic at all! When he came in close, I could feel his breath on me, and my head was going crazy, like I was screaming, 'Shit, shit, shit!' I knew exactly what was going to happen, and then it did. He kissed me.

It was all very rushed and very inappropriate in my eyes. There weren't any massive fireworks going off for me, because I felt so awful about the fact he was married. I couldn't get my head around it, nor could I get my head around how he would then just go home. It was so weird. Was that normal? There was no manual on this, though, and I didn't really know who to turn to.

I called Jenny and was mortified to even have to tell her that I had bloody kissed my landlord! She never judged me, though. She just told me to take each day, and that's what I did.

It was the same advice I took from her many years later.

But from that moment on, whatever started never stopped...

Chapter Fifteen

We started to spend so much time together that I became his right-hand girl, and he would ask my opinions on lots of things. We talked as much as we could on the phone and WhatsApp messages I would see him every day in the yard. It was like we were inseparable.

Slowly but surely, I began to trust him – something I had thought I would never be able to do again – and I started to see that this relationship was so different to anything I had ever experienced before.

And from experiencing no fireworks and not really fancying him, my head along with my heart took a total U-turn. And yes, I fancied him, and yes, there were fireworks.

But, of course, he always had to go home. Watching him walk away time after time was so difficult, and over time my friends would ask me, 'Will he leave her?' or 'How will things work out?' or even 'How the fuck did that happen?' They were questions I never knew the answers to, but I would never have asked him to leave his family. If anything, I assumed it would be me that would have to walk away or make the right choice for us all… probably by walking away.

The simple truth is that we fell in love, and that never changed throughout my time living in the caravan. He made it a better place for me to raise my children, and my gratitude to him will last an eternity. No matter what people think of what he did and how he did things, nothing was ever done through malice. I know that might sound ludicrous, though, because what was happening still wasn't right.

Mr R utterly changed my life – and so did I – and I'll cherish my three years I spent in that caravan forever. Sitting on my fake grass, looking at clear skies, enjoying the silence, and gazing at stars. In my mind, I would see myself with Mr R one day. How? I didn't have a clue. When? How long is a piece of string?

And in those visualisation moments, I would also see myself as the successful businesswoman I longed to be, strong and proud, living a life in which I could fully support myself and my kids financially. My ultimate plan was not to have to borrow or owe money, and to be able to stand on my own two feet.

I shared earlier that Mr R had spoken of his mother who had passed away, and I liked talking about her. She gave me a feeling of strength, just like my nan; I felt like she was on my side, too. My spirituality would come and go during my time at the caravan – more so in my time of need, when the comfort from spirit would step in.

By stepping in, I mean I would be able to hear them, see them, and communicate with them in my mind's eye. I would describe it as having a dream but being awake the whole time, talking to them in my mind, and hearing their replies. It is just as though you had told me you had a conversation in a dream, and you were relaying it back to me. Their communication would help to change how I felt in my time of need, whether that was lifting me when I felt sad, guiding me when I felt confused, or championing me when I did well.

I often felt as if Mr R's mother was beside me. One evening when we had some time together, I described her looks and features to him, and he was shocked at how accurate I was.

She later became the little robin that would visit Mr R's office, or land on my fake grass garden. I just knew it was her, and she would often come close to me on a Sunday.

Let's talk about Sundays…

Sundays were such a hard day for me, as that was Mr R's family day. I longed to have a 'conventional' family, and on those days I felt so alone, spending time with my parents or with Kerry just to take my mind off the fact Mr R was with his family. We didn't talk at all on Sundays, and I couldn't just call him. There were boundaries I had to adhere to.

Now I know you're probably thinking he was a married man, so what did I expect to happen? I don't want sympathy or for anyone to feel bad for me, as I absolutely agree I was caught up in this situation with my eyes wide open. But it still doesn't change how lonely I felt.

I used to keep myself busy with the kids, especially once I had a little more money each month after keeping the caravan rent and bills stable. We would do cinema trips, have cosy film days, and spend Sundays with friends and family. But all the time I was hiding the fact that I felt so lost in my heart. It was Amy performing again, and I would check my phone all the time just in case he could manage to call or text me.

As time went on, Sundays never got easier. If anything, they just got harder and harder. Sunday evenings, after the kids went to bed, I was back to sobbing on my own with the curtains closed. I felt so alone, torn knowing what the right thing was and not being able to walk away from someone I loved.

I have always hidden my pain from the kids, and as we settled into the caravan life, they saw me start to laugh again, to smile and enjoy life! For so long I had been carrying life like an emotional backpack full of struggle, and slowly that backpack was becoming lighter. But Sundays and his family holidays would deeply affect me emotionally.

I'm not going to sit here and say that my mind didn't go crazy thinking about everything he was doing whilst we were apart. You can imagine what was running through my mind, with all the sordid details of the ifs, buts, and maybes of the situation. But I was putting myself through that, and at that stage I never actually blamed Mr R for his part. Ok, he started things between us, but I was free to walk away at any time. Instead, I chose to be loyal to him, and I chose to be alone at those times for him to be with his family.

I knew I had fallen in love with him. When we were together, I would laugh until my belly hurt, talk about life until our mouths went dry, and he would always try and help me move forward with any plans and ideas I had.

He never once made me feel stupid – like someone had done before – nor did he make me feel like a far-out dreamer. He would talk me through my visions and discuss how to make them reality. But while his support and belief without a doubt gave me strength, I had to keep going alone.

Sundays were the days when I would write and rewrite endless messages to him. They always consisted of 'I can't do this any more, please stay at home and leave me out of whatever is missing in your life… blah, blah'. When I was left alone with my thoughts, I just wanted out.

My heart was hurting to watch someone I loved so much walking away to live a whole other life without me, another world, whilst I just had to watch it happen. Looking back, I don't know how I did it for so long. Many of my friends still say they watched me and didn't know how I managed it. My answer now is that I don't know either, but back then it was always 'I have to. This is my choice.' Then I would say, 'One day…' But I didn't know how, and I didn't really want to know how.

No matter what, in my vision for my future, Mr R was always there. One Sunday I was sobbing in my little toilet room, and Mr R's mother was there, her voice as clear as my nan's had been that day at her resting place. As though she was in the room with me, I heard his mother say, 'Please keep going. You can do this.'

Her words never left me, just like my nan's didn't that day Mr R took me to her grave. I trusted his mother and I could feel her picking me up and straightening my crown. She kept saying, 'Keep going.' So that's what I did. That's what I always did.

Chapter Sixteen

During my time in the caravan with Mr R (and without him, which was harder), I felt like I was living a dream. I started to have spare money again, to be able to treat my kids, to be able to enjoy my life for what it was at that time, being able to put my head on my pillow at night knowing the kids were safe and their home was secure. After so many years of struggle and strife, it was a feeling of pure bliss.

Despite my relationship with Mr R and the uncertainty it held, I knew that no matter what happened between us he would never have taken my home from me. And he showed me a different side of life that I never knew existed. At times I felt like Julia Roberts in the film *Pretty Woman* – just without the hooker bit! I guess, sleeping with my landlord, some might say I was a hooker in some ways. Seriously, though, it wasn't like that at all. We created a world that not many people could probably understand, and I always paid my way.

He was the one and only man in my life, but our life together ran parallel to the one he had at home.

Some might describe it as 'nice shirts and nights out' or that 'he was getting from me what she wasn't giving him', but it genuinely ran much deeper than that. He started to become a father figure to my children – something they hadn't had for so long. And I knew I could rely on him most of the time.

I had to get used to being left alone, though. I'd go on holiday alone, go to bed alone, and spent Sundays and special calendar dates on my own. It's funny how you can force a smile and hide the pain of resentment at Christmas, which is my most favourite time of the year. And thoughts of "new year new starts" become questionable when you can't share special times with someone as a couple in a 'normal' relationship without having the shadows of another world following you. I continued to live on the other side of his life. Just me and the kids; it was always us against the world, and me fighting my emotions all the time.

There were times when I wondered if it would be much easier to just be single, as surely there would be less upset. But I couldn't let him go – and neither could he.

Thankfully, Mr R coming and going like a revolving door didn't affect the kids. I didn't lie to them about the fact he had other children to go home to, but we kept the depth of our relationship from them as much as we could. To them he was my 'good friend', but that was my way of protecting them as always.

Just because I was hurting at times, there was no way I wanted them to suffer. For so many years I had hidden my sadness and fear during my relationship with their dad, but this was so different. I had security in the yard, in our caravan, and that's what mattered to them.

Due to the manageable rent I was paying, I was able to have some money left over each month, and I could finally manage to take the kids abroad on holiday myself for the first time.

When I announced that I was taking the kids abroad, everyone freaked out like it was an alien thing to do, me and two kids going to another country alone. I had only ever been abroad with their dad with them in the past, so I'm not going to lie, I did crap myself on the plane. At one point, their dad did try to stop us going, and he threatened to get the police to the airport and say I was kidnapping the children.

I know it sounds ridiculous, but my heart pounded as we passed through security, praying I wasn't going to get dragged away by the police in front of my kids. I still wasn't able to stop his threats unsettling me and causing me anxiety. Even though he'd never paid a penny for them and didn't have any influence in their upbringing, I was angry that he didn't want me to take his children on a beautiful holiday and give them the break they deserved.

We went to a villa in Portugal, which was quiet and safe, and we had an amazing time. I was so proud of myself, but I noticed how free I felt from the torment of Mr R going home every night. There were times when I felt really lonely. I missed being with someone, just chilling in the evening with someone special, the simple things that people have in everyday relationships and don't even notice. I didn't need a man, but I wanted to share my life with someone. Fair enough, the situation with Mr R wasn't ideal in any way, but like a magnet, there was no keeping us apart. Somehow, we just kept going day by day.

I spent three more holidays alone during the time we lived in the caravan. I went to hotels the following times, and it gave me a chance to meet people and the kids to make friends and just be around some holiday hustle and bustle.

Lanzarote became my favourite place to be, as it was so peaceful and friendly, and my love for that place stays with me and the kids now. I would sit on my balcony at night, looking across the sea, listening to the waves, my heart heavy and torn at what to do about Mr R and our relationship. I didn't know if I should carry on or walk away, because he definitely wasn't going to let me go. Yet he had no plan to create any type of future for us or security for me. By security, I don't mean financially; I just mean an active plan to show me there was light at the end of the tunnel.

I often felt as though I was putting my life on hold for him. Again, that wasn't his fault as it was my choice, but I was getting older, and I wanted some kind of plan for my future. I came to realise years later that there was a plan in my mind the whole time, and looking back I often wonder if things would have been different and moved quicker if I had been firmer and not so supportive of his double life. Mr R was a 'live for today' type of guy. If I ever said, 'What do you think will happen?' he would reply, 'I'm getting through today.'

I totally believe that's exactly what he was doing – literally getting through each day. Some of my friends actually felt sorry for him, and at times I did, too. I know my mum did. She could see he loved me and the kids but had to do the right thing for his family.

To anyone else, it wasn't the right thing, and in all honesty the situation was fucking us all over, including him. I used to feel myself screaming in my mind, yearning for him to change things.

But he came from a good place with it; I know he did.

His children are *everything* to him.

If only they knew.

If only they knew what he put himself through to keep up the lie to stay with them.

I never ever asked him to leave them; it wasn't my place to do that. But him 'having his cake and eating it' was difficult for me, and it looked like he was living the dream doing his family thing and looking like he had it all. Then he had me waiting in the wings, who never asked for anything and never demanded answers, despite the questions that would mull round in my head on the quiet.

We laughed, we joked, and when he needed someone to talk to, I supported him unconditionally. Some would say I gave him all the good stuff.

But I can see now how bloody stressful it all was for him. And as for just sharing the good stuff, our relationship was so much more than that.

Chapter Seventeen

While we were in Lanzarote, he would go on his family holidays. So, holidays were bittersweet for me, knowing as I watched him walk away to go on his holiday that he would be her husband.

That probably sounds daft, because I knew they were together. But somehow, I coped better when he was in the yard working and we were able to communicate. His holidays were like three weeks of Sundays, basically. If he could call, he would, but it would be for five minutes max, if that. Or he would send a quick text when he could. Some days I wouldn't hear from him at all.

I would go away on my holiday at the same time, as for some strange reason it helped me cope better when I was away, too. I would set myself challenges not to take my phone out with me. I would leave it in the room so that I would miss his calls and texts to make myself seem less available, but then I would be annoyed at myself for playing silly games.

I would get through the days with the children poolside, beachside, or going for a walk, temporarily freeing myself of my mixed-up emotions. But when it was quiet or I had time on my own, my imagination would run wild, and I would sometimes make myself physically sick.

It would always bring me back on my balcony, listening to the waves and watching the sea, breathing in and out, blowing my thoughts away with the ocean.

No matter where we both were, we would always say that the moon connected us. Our worlds were one.

We would send pictures to each other of the moon from our destinations, and for those brief moments we would feel close again. The message was always, 'Look at the moon.' If anyone asked why I was on holiday alone with two kids, I would make up a story of how my partner was taking his children on holiday, that we weren't a blended family as yet, so he did his thing, and I did mine. I had the story planned out and would sugar-coat the whole thing. I'm sure they would say behind my back that something wasn't right, but it felt better for me to embellish the whole story and make out I was totally ok with it. I would tell it in such a breezy way, sounding so sure that I was 'fine'. It was sort of true, but only sort of. I just left out the part that there was another family thrown in and I wasn't ok with that, but other people didn't have to know.

I would sit on holiday watching other families, wondering if there were secrets or complications behind their stories. And I would read so many books to stop my imagination running wild with the thoughts of his family holiday, what they were all doing, how, what, where, who…

I met some lovely people during my time away, and I thank them for their friendship during my holidays. I have kept in touch with a few of them, and I definitely think they will either say they knew something wasn't right, or be really shocked at the depth of my story. On those warm evenings, we would all be laughing and joking with the kids, having drinks, but I had to hide the sadness I felt when I went back to the room alone to look at the moon.

If you feel like yelling, *Amy, what were you doing?*

please let me explain. It wasn't like I had to have a man to keep me going, or needed anything from a man other than love and friendship. It was just that I knew I didn't come first.

In the past, I had been second to alcohol and control, and at times this relationship with Mr R brought up similar feelings, even though our situation was totally different. I was living in the shadows; the other woman, you may say. I questioned all the time how the hell I had got myself into this, how I was going to get myself out of it, if I really did have that much little self-respect, and then wonder if and why I wasn't good enough for him to just get his shit sorted, make sure his family were ok, and put me first.

My holidays with my kids became my therapy. I never wanted to leave the freedom of the sea view and the comfort of the moon. I just wanted normal. But I couldn't ask that of him..

I always came home from holidays with a plan to walk away, but as soon as I walked into the airport and he would be there waiting for us, the love would come rushing through me again. I loved him so much, and he felt the same, if not more. I honestly feel he loved me more than he ever knew was possible. He didn't want to lose me or let me go, but not in the controlling way I had experienced in the past.

One thing he proved throughout the time since I met him was that, despite the shit situation, he was as genuine as he could be. If I needed help, he would try his utmost to help; if I needed advice, he was there; if I needed anything and he wasn't there, he would make sure someone else was. The people in the yard would step up for me if Mr R couldn't — and when I say he couldn't, I mean if he was at home. One time, I broke down on the M25 and it was a Sunday! Bloody Sundays! But he sent someone to sort me out.

Me and the kids were wrapped in tinfoil on the hard shoulder of the motorway, and I was pissed off to the max, thinking about him sitting all cosy eating his cheese and biscuits. But someone came to rescue us, and he was the one who organised that. Now I can see clearly that he did what he could, despite my feelings of resentment at the time. I guess it's easy to feel more at peace with things when you're out of the situation, isn't it? Clarity comes with time.

If I was out on a night out, he would send his driver to come and pick me up, and said driver would do multiple drop-offs to ensure all my friends got home safely. The driver and neighbour became a friend for life to me and the kids

winter was tough, both practically and emotionally. On the occasions when it would snow and my pipes in the caravan would ice over, I couldn't help being totally pissed off at the thought of Mr R having a lovely hot shower in his beautiful big house.

We did manage to get the opportunity to travel together a few times during those three years, and the places we saw and the experiences we shared definitely gave me that *Pretty Woman* feeling. When I was standing at the top of the Burj Khalifa in Dubai, or the Leaning Tower of Pisa, or watching bullfighting in Portugal, or having dinner in London's west end, that little girl from the caravan was more worthy than she knew.

I would wait all year for one overnight stay, and as the years rolled by I longed for 'normal'. I wanted to cook dinner for him, then go to bed and wake up next to him. Even the 'what are we having for dinner?' conversation seemed attractive. And by then the hotel stays, the trips, and the date nights weren't so fun any more.

Our relationship routine had become really regimented. I had certain evenings roughly 3 times a week when I would settle the kids to bed, and he would come to the caravan. We would have dinner together, chill and watch a film, and then... I'm pretty sure you know the rest.

Chapter Eighteen

I'd had a massive issue with sleep since the day I left the kids' dad. I could maybe manage a few hours here and there, but I struggled. I would lie awake for hours and hours, wondering if this was it for me, watching someone I loved walking away to go and get in bed with someone else. I would feel the pain in my chest rising as I kept thinking about it. Often, I would end up watching films to keep me going through the night, ready for the next day.

But when Mr R came over, I would snuggle up to him and feel such contentment. I had him there temporarily, just us, but I didn't want to sleep then, or the night would be over – something I dreaded every single time.

Most people think that if you're having an affair, it's all raunchy hotel nights. But it wasn't like that for us, and our overnight opportunities were rare. We would stay out if we could on a few occasions, but again I was so desperate to have these moments that I didn't want to sleep and miss a single minute of being with him before we had to return to reality. If I could have put matchsticks in my eyes, I would have!

As time went on and the years went by, there were fewer overnight trips – not that the lack of trips or hotel stays directly bothered me. It was the quality time together I missed, no matter where it was.

The 'routine' began to wobble a little into year four, and I would go weeks without having any 'alone' time with him at all. On several occasions, I might book a table for us to go out on a Saturday date night, only for his home life to announce plans at the last minute – so I was dropped. I could be all dressed up and ready to go out, waiting on him arriving, when a text would come through:

I can't make it. I'll call you tomorrow.

I couldn't call him because he was at home. And I knew if I sent him a text, he wouldn't be able to reply. And this started to happen a lot.

Despite how we felt about each other, it's important for me to make clear that he always put his family first the best he could. But I was starting to find it so tough.

I started to turn to my psychic friends, people I'd had readings with in the past. I guess I went to them during this time because all I wanted was someone to tell me 'yes, he is going to make the choice' and 'yes, you're doing the right thing standing by him'.

The very few psychics I trusted all said the same thing: you will be together, and he does love you. None of them knew how or when, but they always told me it was going to be tough and a very long road.

Two of my psychic friends, Suzanne and Nicole, saved me from my own mind talk with their constant guidance and reassurance! But I came to realise that deep down I knew the answers already, and so did my nan and Mr R's mum.

I was just becoming scared all the time that I was going to have to be the one who walked away, because no matter how much I knew we were soulmates, I just couldn't see him being able to leave his other life.

I was a woman in my thirties, so this wasn't a playground situation or some puppy love. I craved to be one of those normal families I would see on holiday, deciding what colour the bathroom should be painted or watching rubbish on TV. Everything that so many couples would see as boring or mundane, that was all I wanted. It was never about money.

The craving for 'normal' was verging on desperate in my mind. We were heading into year four and nothing had changed in terms of his situation, but I knew I was changing. I wanted so much more, but I was in no position to ask. I wouldn't, and he never had any answers, no plans, and to him tomorrow was another day.

I started to experience more sad days than good, more anger than joy, just one big ball of pain. It became so hard; too hard at times. I was trying to cling on and appreciate the good times, but any time I tried to make plans, his famous words were: 'We will see.' But that was what my parents used to say when I was younger, and when they did they really meant 'no'!

Chapter Nineteen

Finally, after three years and five months of living in the caravan – originally meant to be a six-month pit-stop – we were moving to a house! I was taking my kids to live in a beautiful house, in a new town in Hertfordshire, with amazing schools.

Jasmine was getting older, so I had it in my mind that if I was going to make the move, then I should try to do it soon. The kids, though, were more than happy to stay in the caravan. They both loved living there, and I always encouraged them to be proud of what we had.

I remember one day Jasmine was at school and a girl was taking the piss, saying, 'You live in a caravan. Your mum has no money.' When Jasmine told me, I was livid that a kid could be so cruel. I had explained to her that not everyone has to be liked and you should own your power in your own skin. In this case, Jasmine did just that, as she told me, 'Don't worry, Mum, they are just jealous. Everyone wants to live in a caravan.'

I did laugh, but I still marched down to the school with steam coming out of my ears, barged my way through a crowded reception, and demanded an explanation. Truth is, I didn't get one. Kids are kids, aren't they? But I was so protective of the fact I was doing everything I could to provide and put a roof over their heads.

Keeping them in the same school since day one had always been my mission, but I could see that Reggie was losing his way. He didn't enjoy school, and he wasn't getting his needs met at the one they went to. As Jasmine was such a clever girl, I didn't want her efforts wasted, so I took the massive decision to move them both. It was a difficult decision, which made me extremely anxious, and I really battled with my demons over whether I was doing the right thing or not.

Moving my kids to a beautiful house, and giving them a better education, how was I not doing the right thing? But I was shitting it. We would be leaving the bubble of the yard, walking away from the caravan – the only place I felt at home. It was so scary.

The house I found was stunning, and before we moved in I had it decorated beautifully with their choice of wallpaper in their bedrooms. It was set in a quiet cul-de-sac, and the schools were, as I had researched, outstanding.

I should have felt on top of the world that my life was finally changing, but I had a feeling in the pit of my stomach I just couldn't shift. I was terrified of leaving the security blanket that the caravan had become.

January 2018, and I was sitting on the floor of a hotel in Disneyland Paris. I had surprised the kids with the trip to Disney – a dream come true for me, as it was somewhere I'd always wanted to visit. I did so much research before we went, joining chat groups on Facebook to make sure that the kids wouldn't miss out on a thing. My solo adventure with my little dream team turned out to be breath-taking, and I cried happy tears the whole time!

Yet at the back of my mind, I knew that we'd be leaving the caravan in less than two weeks, and when the kids were asleep in their Disney beds, my anxiety would creep in, and I would be sitting on the floor freaking out. I should have been soaking up every second of that trip, but when the kids were sleeping, I was exhausted, shaking, and worrying myself sick about the house move. Would it be ok? Would I be able to sustain it? Would I be able to afford it all? I was so afraid of losing everything again, and knew I couldn't go through the shepherd's pie syndrome. My body wouldn't take it, and nor could my mental health.

My parents weren't thrilled either. I think they wanted me to stay at the caravan because it was safe, and because they had seen me happy again. But it couldn't be forever. It was never a life plan, and the yard wasn't the place to bring up the kids long-term.

Mr R reassured me I was doing the right thing and that the schools alone were the right reason to move. I knew he was right, and one thing he never did was encourage me to fail. He knew I was strong and believed I was invincible. But when he told me not to worry, I felt that was so easy for him to say. He had his family, and he had me who adored him! Nothing was changing for him.

The day we left the caravan, I cried so much. I felt like I was being pushed and pulled to keep going, taking each step to make the move happen. I hated it, but I knew the move had to be made, so I pushed through the boundaries of fear.

One of the upsides was that I was finally able to have a bath, after over three years. The shower in the caravan was tiny, and during my time there I missed soaking in a nice, long bath. It's weird to think now I hate baths, but I still have a photo my friend took of me lying, fully clothed, in the bath in the new house that first day. I'm sure she knew that behind my smile I was hiding so much fear! Change was always so hard, and I'd always associated it with loss, but this move had to be done for the kids and their future.

Another reason I was worried about the move was that it would no longer be 'convenient' for me and Mr R to spend any time together. Our time was already running low at that point, and moving meant I would no longer be around the yard at his workplace, where I could at least catch a glimpse of him or chat for a few minutes. Thinking about it now, it turns my stomach that I was so happy just to have a few minutes of his time, and I would cling onto that until the next time. How pathetic is that!

But I was thinking of my the future, and this was a long game.

The move of school changed Reggie's life and saved my little boy from being lost in the world of education. He wasn't naughty or disruptive on purpose, and never rude, but he had so much energy, his concentration span was minimal, and he just needed the right support. Having been brought up in a working yard of men, lorries, and outdoors, he really didn't want to be in school. To be fair, I got it.

The old school didn't channel his qualities right or understand him, but his new one did. They took his cheeky personality and his love of sport and the outdoors, and they channelled it in the right way to fuel him to learn in the classroom.

Jasmine didn't have a space to be in the same school as Reggie, so he went alone for four months. It was tough, because although there are four years between them, they hadn't been separated before, and two different schools wasn't ideal for me either. As a single mum, I couldn't be in two different places. So for those four months I home-schooled Jasmine while I fought to get her a place at Reggie's school, then took it to an appeal which I won. That's when our new life officially began.

The kids quickly made lovely friends, and everyone was so nice – but really posh. I felt as though I stuck out like a sore thumb – the Essex redhead who had lived in a caravan, surrounded by 'Cheshire housewives'. These mums definitely had their shit together, and they all seemed older than me, but they were friendly and they made time to talk to me.

I kept myself to myself a lot and didn't make friends for ages, but I was digging my heels in where I didn't need friends. I had my friends in Essex, so I didn't need new ones in Hertfordshire. I had only made the move so that the kids could have a better education; it wasn't about me.

The only person I knew who lived in that town was Mr R. It was him who had drawn my attention to the fact that the schooling there was outstanding, and suggested that maybe it was time I made the move for the children.

However, I was unsure how our relationship would continue, particularly when I was no longer so 'convenient' – not a nice word.

Mr R always said the move wouldn't change anything… but the move changed everything.

Chapter Twenty

We spent one year in that house, and although I still supposedly had my Mr R routine – three evenings – it soon became more apparent that it was less than that. It would be hit and miss, to be honest. I wasn't sure why, because he drove past my house to go home from the yard, so surely he could have dropped in to say hello? But then, didn't I want more than just a few minutes of his time?

I'd had this idea that the house would make us more 'family-like', and he could spend time there, so I gave him a key and initially it made me feel like we were moving forward. But money started to become tight again, which sent me into a panic, and I immediately began to regret the move. In truth, I never slept in my bedroom, and when I say never, it was *never*. I always slept on the sofa. I still had the sleeping issues, and that house didn't cure them.

As you can imagine, moving from a caravan into a four-bedroom house was a shock to the system financially, and I don't doubt anyone would have found this a challenging time. But as always, the pressure came on me – and just me. I often wondered what it would feel like to be in a relationship where responsibilities and concerns were shared. What the hell did that feel like?

The pressure never left me, but I know now it was sent to try me, to the point where it made me driven. It gave me more ambition, and the hunger inside me to be a success for the children was everything that kept me going. I wanted them to know that I was always busting my balls for them and to give them a good life.

As times got harder and emotions became more painful, my friends would ask how I got through the days with this Mr R situation, but it was my kids that got me through my days and nights, just as they had when I was struggling with their dad. And even though I couldn't guarantee what would happen to me and Mr R, or how that would end, I couldn't stop loving him – and the feelings were very mutual.

It was so fucked up at times with how happy we were and how normal we looked. But watching someone you love walk away time and time again, and just accepting it, that's not normal.

This house –the house I had longed for to create the set-up my kids deserved –just wasn't how it should have felt. I missed the caravan and everything about it so much, it was like I was grieving. My mum would ask if I missed the caravan, and I would just say I couldn't talk about it because it upset me so much. I missed the caravan, I missed Mr R, and I missed the hustle and bustle of the yard. As I said before, it was like a world that most people didn't know existed; a family, but not through blood.

In the new house, the kids weren't used to being so far apart, and for ages they didn't like being upstairs on their own. So, we got walkie-talkies they could use until we all got used to the distance of upstairs and downstairs.

I spent every night lying with Reggie in his room until he fell asleep, then I'd lie with Jasmine watching films in her bed. The kids would comfort me without knowing it, and they gave me hope on the many occasions when I thought there was none.

I felt like I was slowly sinking again money-wise, and I was frustrated, angry, and hurt that this might happen again. Little did I know that my fears were feeding that vision. I was creating them in a negative way, and that's the energy I was feeding in. I didn't know then what I know now, that focusing on fear in your mind creates the reality you hold in your hand – whether that was about money or my relationship with Mr R changing.

And of course, all of those fears happened!

However, during the one year in that house, three blessings happened in my life.

I was still doing beauty , but I had moved away from all my clients, and it was impossible financially for me to keep travelling back to do their nails and brows. My beauty treatments, though, were all I had to keep us afloat somehow, and sitting around not trying just wasn't me.

Again, I turned to my psychic network for guidance. There was one girl, Nicole, who I hadn't even met in real life, but the power of social media and spirit had done their work by bringing us together. We had become such good friends, supporting each other and exchanging words of wisdom. We trusted each other implicitly and knew we were only a text away when the other needed help.

Nicole had a growing online following for psychic readings, but her work was starting to overwhelm her, and she became unwell. As she had so many simple psychic email readings already booked in, she asked me to do some for her. You might think this was a big jump, and a big chance, away from beauty. But as I've explained already, I had always known there was more to me and my psychic abilities.

Nicole saw this and she trusted it. She knew I was capable. She knew I had the ability. I kept telling her I was unsure, and I knew I would have to build up my confidence, but she threw me in at the deep end. And like any entrepreneur out there, what do we do when in doubt? We jump in headfirst, take every opportunity we are given, and we fucking run with it!!

I spoke to my aunt, who has always championed me, and she told me to go for it. She had every faith that I could do it, too. It was only ten-question reads, which involved Nicole's clients emailing a question on which they wanted psychic guidance. It could be love, life, career, finances, or what the future would bring. My job was to use my psychic intuition to connect to their energy and write a short reply. I felt nervous, but at the same time I felt guided that this was the right thing for me – and the little bit of extra money would undoubtedly be helpful.

I sat on my sofa, with my crystals for protection, and started to read the individual question from each client. This enabled me to create an energy exchange with each and every one of them.

I noticed as I was reading that I would call instinctively on my ability to connect to spirit, and they would give me information and detail. I could clearly hear the guidance being given to me for each specific client – something called Clairaudience – and this was combined with feelings within my body – known as Clairsentience. These abilities helped me to read online and to offer my services to a high standard and with impeccable accuracy.

I trusted what I was doing, in the same way that I had trusted my nan and Mr R's mum. And as time went on, I learned to trust it more and I learned to listen more. My aunt guided me with her knowledge, and she became my mentor as my psychic business began.

I had always been in awe of businesswomen around me, like Vicki and her mum, Kim. During those dark days with the kids' dad, I would go to Kim's house – two kids in tow – to do her nails, and she would be constantly making big plans. I would look at her and feel her energy. I kept saying, 'When I grow up, I want to be Kim Antoniou.' But at that time, I was a 25-year-old mother of two young kids, with very little voice left in me, my confidence dropping, crying more than I was smiling, so I didn't feel very grown up.

As my confidence grew with the psychic readings, I set up my own page on social media, joined a psychic group to offer readings, became an approved reader, and the clients started to roll in thick and fast. My name began to be mentioned all over the place, online on apps, psychic pages, and so many other platforms. My inbox was flooded daily, and I was reading online all day and night!

During this time, I developed my confidence to be able to bring loved ones from spirit to those on earth – otherwise known as mediumship. And that is how Amy Fleckney Mediumship was born.

Every single one of my clients I read for matters to me. I care so much about each of them and being able to connect to their loved ones and bring words of comfort. Each time I do a reading, it's like the first one all over again; I feel the same rush of adrenaline and experience the same shock at my own abilities.

I became more disciplined to be able to work with spirit, and from that moment on my expectations of what I expected from them grew. I promised them I would always work to the highest of my ability for them – a mutual agreement between me and spirit.

As my business took off, I vowed to do my very best. And with my aunt by my side supporting me, and my psychic network helping me, I knew I was looked after with my development. I also joined a small local circle to keep developing more. Just like the times I'd visited spiritual churches when I was younger, I really enjoyed being around other mediums.

The difference was, though, now I wasn't just looking up to them in awe. I was one.

Chapter Twenty-one

I felt like I really belonged. I finally fitted, and I was confident in the knowledge that I loved who I was becoming. It was as though the penny had finally dropped!

I was actually ready to be who I had always been. Just like the day when I knew my dad's aunt had passed and I was able to feel her around me, I was ready to use my ability to help people. It was that simple. That is when my mission statement was born: 'All I want to do is help people, heal some grief in their hearts, and provide for my kids.'

And that is exactly what I did.

Straight away, I was making a difference to all kinds of people and in various places around the world. One connection I'll never forget was a reading I did for a lady in Canada. Her son had taken his life at a young age, and he connected with me. It was life-changing for her to be able to connect to him again, and for me to be able to bring all of him through, describing his looks and all his personality traits. We also touched on some details of his passing, as well as his life on earth. He had been a talented artist, and I was lucky enough to see some of his artwork, which he shared with me during the connection i had with him. His mum said she felt like I had him in the same room as me – a feeling she had been missing for so long.

It was this read that made me realise that what I was doing was life-changing for people. I know some people don't believe, and that's their choice. But trust me, there is no way I could ever know that that random lady in Canada, with a private social media account, had a son who was amazing at art, was in spirit with his best friend (who unfortunately had taken his life shortly after), and could describe everything from the clothes he was wearing to the inside of her house the day she found him. I couldn't make that up.

It's like running a film clip in my third eye, or my mind, if you want to think of it like that. I can hear, I can feel, and spirit show themselves in my mind. It's like the dream feeling I mentioned, except that I'm awake and I'm able to ask questions in my mind.

I was honoured that the Canadian lad had come through to me, and I was truly grateful that I was able to give his mum the comfort she needed with his message to her. From that moment, I knew I had a huge responsibility to be the best communicator I could be for spirit. My expectation of myself was high already, and it just keeps getting higher.

And I wasn't scared! It felt so right!

This is it Amy… this is you!

Mr R wasn't a believer, and he wasn't really in tune with his spiritual side, but he was always supportive and intrigued by what I could for people. He didn't even seem shocked with my business transition from beauty therapist to psychic. It seemed such a natural switch, and he could see I was making something of it.

Part of me also felt like he was pleased that I had a distraction from our relationship, which had never had an end line or a plan. And to be fair, my work *was* a distraction for me. I threw myself into growing my client base, and I lived and breathed my business. I still do.

Funnily enough, I would sit in my car and do readings online, because I preferred being in my car than at the house. I still didn't enjoy that house at all, as it didn't feel like home. And for some reason, my car has always been my therapy room – now it was also my office!

Mr R's mum wasn't around me as much when we lived in that house. By that I mean she rarely connected to me directly, but the little robin always came most days, and I felt guided to believe that the robin was her continuing to give me that strength to believe. I would look out my kitchen window at the small and uninviting garden, but when she came as the robin and sat on the outside bench, I always felt comforted, and I drew strength from it.

I knew she wanted me to keep believing in her son, and I did believe that everything would turn out for the good. I later learnt that she had been a very successful and strong businesswoman herself. Her story is all so familiar to my own vision, so maybe her presence was more than just connected to Mr R and she saw something in me that I didn't. Of course, she did!

Life was settling down. The kids were doing well at the new school, and I was working on myself and my business, which was going from strength to strength with clients from all over the world.

Becoming an approved reader within a psychic group, alongside some other readers, definitely helped me reach out to clients and to give me endless practice. It is also how Scottish Gemma came into my life, as we became close friends through the group. Later, we set up on our own group with a few more readers we let in, and that group is still going strong today with members all over the world and growing daily.

Many of the clients have been ladies who are going through fertility issues or some sort of fertility journey, trying to conceive. So, I soon found myself specialising in fertility reads, predicting pregnancy, baby genders, and the details of their pregnancy journey. With the help of spirit and my accurate high quality psychic intuition, the predictions were flowing correctly, and the success rate was getting higher. I loved being able to give people hope and support with their fertility and pregnancy journey, and so many of the stories really touched my heart.

My kids are everything to me, and even though my baby days were done, I could see why these women were so desperate to become parents.

At that stage, everything was finally falling into place. Me and Mr R still had a long way to go, of course, but the kids were settled and my business was growing, along with my confidence. For the first time in a long time, I had hope for the future and trusted that everything would work out okay. But, as I was soon to discover, the universe had a big surprise in store.

Chapter Twenty-two

The blue line!!!

'Shit!' was the first word that sprang to mind! I frantically Googled what happens if you're pregnant by a married man – how stupid was that? Imagine turning to Google. But then, Google doesn't judge, and who the hell was going to understand this?

I was freaking out about how the hell I was going to tell my mum and dad after they had supported me so much. Me and the kids were a threesome, and it was all I knew, and all my family had known. Some people might have thought Mr R was going to move in then, but he was married, so we weren't going to run off into the sunset with the kids. There was no way he was going to drop everything because I was pregnant – nor would I have expected him to.

So… Google's response, if you're interested, was: Don't get pregnant by a married man! Great advice, Google. I'm pretty sure in my case it was too bloody late.

But hang on. Google was actually saying: Don't ever get pregnant on purpose by a married man, because he still won't leave his wife! Well, no shit, Sherlock!

I had been a single mum with two kids for six years, and it clearly hadn't been a walk in the park, so there's absolutely no way I would have planned to become a single mum to three kids, with two fathers!

At that moment, I felt overwhelming guilt for Jasmine and Reggie, as I had just been starting to build something to give us stability, and now this.

For so long I'd had to be strong and to keep going, but where would I find the strength to cope now? My pot of strength was running low. I'd got used to the pitying looks from other people all those years before when we moved into the caravan, but it wasn't something I wanted to face again. This shit was getting real, and my contraception had let me down.

Despite my shock and fears, from that second onwards I knew deep down that I would be keeping the baby. I would be lying if I said I didn't have any doubts, but keeping the baby was never really the question for me. I always knew that, and those friends and family who stood by me knew that, too. It was just a really difficult decision to make, because I knew I would be going it alone.

Being a mum is everything to me, and for a long time in my life it was all I felt I was actually good at. It's certainly been the one thing that always kept me going when life has been hard.

I told very few people about the pregnancy initially, and went into a denial stage where I just carried on as if it wasn't happening. Obviously, I looked after myself, but I couldn't talk about it, and I was scared to tell the kids in case they were upset. We were a team, and it had been the three of us for so long, so I was worried how I would cope. But I was older and wiser (well, I hoped I was, though some would say that was debatable!), I was getting settled, and my business was growing. I worked every spare minute I had, taking advantage of my sleepless nights to read for clients in America and Australia, then back to doing UK readings in the daytime. I made sure all time zones were covered if I was awake.

You might be wondering when or how I came to tell Mr R about the baby. The truth is that I put it off for ages, because I was terrified of opening up to him for the very first time since we'd met. I was used to telling him everything, but this was so different. Google had suggested that it was a common thing for the 'other woman' in a relationship to do when there was no plan or end line in sight, but I never wanted him to think I had done this on purpose. In my case, that would have been a risky game to play, and this whole situation was hard enough without bringing an innocent child into it, one who would potentially have to watch its dad walk away night after night to go home to his other children.

The more I thought about that scenario, the more selfish I felt for even thinking it was ok to continue the pregnancy. But choosing to end it would have taken a chunk of me that I wasn't sure I would recover from. I won't lie when I say that I struggled with my decision for the entire nine months. I had no clue how this was going to end, or what the future held for me and Mr R.

When I told Sally and Kerry, both of them were so happy for me. They could see the logic in the whole thing wasn't ideal, but they both made it sound so easy when they told me, 'You are an amazing mum, Amy,' 'You're the strongest person I know,' and 'You can do this.' They also knew how much I loved Mr R and that our relationship, despite its obvious difficulties, was so important to me and that I wasn't giving up on us.

I finally chose to tell Mr R on a lunch date. Like a schoolgirl having to tell her boyfriend something, I was a nervous wreck. But I'd kept putting it off again and again, and I was by then around eight weeks' pregnant, so I knew I had to tell him.

As always, my time with him was so precious and so limited that I hated to drop the bombshell, and I knew it wasn't going to be an easy conversation. I'm not a fool. We stood in the car park after our lunch date, and he was already sitting in his car ready to drive off, while I stood beside the car.

And that seemed the perfect moment to tell him. Part of me thinks that I did that so that he could drive off if he wanted to, and I wouldn't have to deal with his reaction. And to be honest, that's pretty much what he did.

He didn't say much at all. He simply did his usual, went back to the yard to work, and we didn't talk about it much more even on my routine three evening meetings. Our time together had become less and less, the days more mixed, and his visits were more like a quick pop in and out. The pregnancy was rarely mentioned.

It felt as though if we didn't talk about it, we didn't have to face it, which I know sounds awful and very sad. It was such a lonely place for me. I know I had amazing people around me who would always be there for me and the kids, but ultimately, they had their own families, husbands, and partners.

The thought of being a single mum to three kids… wow! No wonder I was speechless most of the time throughout my pregnancy. And clearly Mr R was terrified, which was made clear by the fact we didn't talk about it.

All the feelings I had been experiencing about having a child watch its dad walk away every night, go away on holiday every year, I know those thoughts would have gone through Mr R's head too. He was and is an amazing father to all of his kids, but this was a shit show for him. It's one thing having an affair, but another having a real child involved.

I don't remember when, but at one point we did have a conversation about me ending the pregnancy, which of course would have been the easiest option for him and made the problem go away. However, I would have been left to pick up the pieces of my mental health and emotional well-being, and that was something I definitely wasn't willing to face. So, I made it very clear to him that keeping the baby wouldn't change anything for him; the baby was mine, I would be raising three kids on my own, and I didn't expect anything from him.

I never expected him to leave family just because I was pregnant, nor did I want him to think I would lean on him financially. I made a promise that day to him that I wouldn't demand or expect anything and, most of all, nor would I tell his family! And it is a promise I kept.

I took the hardest route. But I did so with the constant support of my close friends, my psychic network, one of my sisters, and my business. I got through each day – fuck knows how, but again I did.

In the meantime, Mr R and I carried on as though nothing had changed, and the ignorance of it was bliss. I still hadn't told my kids, even when the three of us went on holiday to Turkey that year. I was extremely anxious in case I took ill when we were away, but I didn't want them to miss out on anything, and thankfully we had a good holiday.

I knew I couldn't keep off telling them that I was pregnant, but I was worried that they would be upset at the news – and yes, they were!

Finally, when I was almost seven months' pregnant with my mini bump, my friend Elaine supported me as I told them, and Jasmine cried while Reggie just copied her. As they both sobbed, all Jasmine kept saying was that everything was going to change. I reassured her over and over that it would be fine, and I also found myself reassuring them that Mr R loved them both very much and this wouldn't change anything. Although my relationship with him was becoming strained, I needed them to understand that was not in any way a reflection of them or how he felt about them. He loved them, and for years he had stepped up as a father figure for them.

In Jasmine's case, she had done sex education at school, so I'm sure it freaked her out that it meant me and Mr R had had sex to bring this baby into our lives. And I can laugh now, as I'm sure that was part of the issue for her.

By point in the pregnancy, I was struggling emotionally and crying a lot. I would sit weeping on my kitchen floor, where I knew the kids wouldn't hear me. I felt like the pregnancy was torturing me, not the baby, but the feelings and swirl of hormones were playing havoc with my mental health.

I was trapped in a world of pain. I wanted Mr R to reassure me everything would be ok, just as he had done all those years before when I moved into the caravan… but this time he couldn't, and he didn't.

My parents still didn't know about the pregnancy. I wore baggy jumpers when I went to see them, and my fluffy coat, and I just leaned on the support system of my friends when I needed to. While they, and my sister, helped and supported me, I knew they couldn't really understand what I was going through or how I alone I felt.

Mr R never spoke about the baby. When he came over and I was cuddling up to him, I knew he must have felt the baby kick and the movement rippling through my tummy. But he never mentioned or acknowledged it. I felt so bad that he felt trapped, but I was trapped, too.

As always, though, I carried on. I went to all my appointments and my scans alone, except one. I even went for a 4D scan on my own, where I got to see how much the baby looked like Mr R.

In all that time, I never found out the baby's gender; to me, it didn't matter. I would cuddle my bump, and my intuition always reassured me I would be ok. We would be ok.

I was just scared of bringing the baby into the collided worlds I was living in, and I was consumed with guilt. Fuck, it was all so painful.

Chapter Twenty-three

The one bright spot in this turbulent time happened when I was around four-and-a-half months' pregnant. I was struggling with the situation, and the emotion of it all was getting to me when I poured my heart out to one of my friends as we sat in her kitchen.

Suddenly my phone rang, and although I didn't know the number, I felt guided to answer.

'Amy? It's Sue,' said the person on the line. 'I've seen your name on the system. Would you like me to look after you?'

I knew straight away whose voice that was. Sue had previously been my midwife when I'd had Jasmine (including the twin days) and Reggie. She knew my story with their dad, and we had got on so well in the past with my pregnancies and after-care. I loved her, and I immediately starting crying, 'Yes!' It was as though an angel had been sent to look after me.

I was completely open to her about my situation with Mr R, and she taught me to focus on me and the baby. She also helped me deal with how upset Jasmine was, but thankfully, Reggie was fine with it. Sue was my rock; she was my angel number two of three.

One of my biggest concerns was whether Mr R might not be with me at the birth. I asked all my psychic friends constantly – Nicole especially, and Sue all the time. But none of them had the answer; only Mr R. I just wanted someone to tell me that he was going to be there for me, as I didn't want to do that bit without him. But as time went on, I had to prepare myself that I would just have to deal with it.

Going round and round in my head was the thought that he'd never let me down and had always stood by me. Surely he wouldn't let me do this without him… or would he?

When I said Sue was my angel number two, angel number one had already come into my life during my time in that house..

I needed a lovely babysitter, someone who could sit with Jasmine and Reggie, to play with them and look after them if I was out with friends or Mr R on date nights. I thought a nice young girl would be perfect, and that turned out to be Ella – a beautiful teenage girl, well-spoken and well educated, and with so much wisdom. Before long, she became part of my family, like a surrogate daughter, added-on sister, and best friend rolled into one.

Ella supported me more than I feel she will ever know, and nothing was too much trouble for her – paid or unpaid. She even helped me not be alone on nights when Mr R had family events, and she would come and sit with me. One night in particular – Christmas 2018, when I was nine months' pregnant – he was at some London family shindig, and she and I sat stalking him on social media like crazy lunatics. But she took all the pain away momentarily by just being there. She was so excited about the baby, as she had never been part of a pregnancy journey before. And although she was only 19, she was just so much older than her years and an incredible role model for my children. Ella stole a piece of my heart that she can keep forever.

She came to my 20 weeks' scan with me, never asked me questions, but just listened and supported me. She would tell Jasmine what being a big sister would mean, and how she had loved every second when her own little sister had been born. It helped me so much to know that Jasmine wasn't worrying that this big change was going to be a bad one.

I am sure I had spirit to thank for sending me both these angels to look after me, and for them to play their role somehow.

As time went on, I eventually started to buy things in preparation for the baby's arrival. I had been putting it off for so long that Kerry would be on my arse saying, 'Have you got this yet? Have you got that yet?' It was as though I was in complete denial about the fact there was a baby coming.

It was so difficult to get excited because I felt like I was losing Mr R slowly every day. Physically, he was still around, but emotionally he seemed numb to the fact there was going to be a baby here any day. We didn't go out any more as my bump grew, I stopped going to the yard, and we just spent the odd evening in together.

I was trying to understand the situation from his point of view all the time whilst juggling my kids and my business, but I had enough to contend with battling my own emotions without trying to work out his as well. There were times when I wanted to be so hard on him, and I'd snap, 'You know what, it's totally fine. You go with your family. I've said I'm doing this alone, so I am. Bye!'

But again, it always came back to me loving him, and I'd try to see things from his point of view. I had to. What rights did I have? I wasn't married to him. I knew my place.

At 33 weeks, I finally told my parents and my family that I was pregnant. It sounds daft a 34-year-old woman hiding a pregnancy from her family, but I didn't want to worry anyone, and I was struggling. My mum was upset, and I felt bad for shutting her out, but my sister reassured her that this had to be done my way.

As the birth date grew nearer, I was desperate to find out my baby's gender. And although predicting baby genders every day was part of my psychic work, I just couldn't work out my own. I just knew the baby couldn't be born on a Sunday, and that I desperately wanted Mr R to be there with me.

While I knew it was a distinct possibility he wouldn't be there, I clung to the hope that he might, and my head was screaming for reassurance. When I would say things randomly like 'You will be there, won't you?' he wouldn't answer. I guess he didn't make promises he couldn't keep, and I had already promised that I would not expect or demand anything from him.

For several years he had had to lie to people he loved just to be somewhere else. I hated the lies, but this was one time when I wanted to beg him to lie just to be with me.

Towards the end of my pregnancy, I became unwell with a water infection, and I was in agony. Going for a wee felt as though I was on fire, and I felt sick and faint so much of the time. I spent long days in the hospital, while they checked the baby's heart rate and pains in my tummy. And when I wasn't at the hospital, I was still working while Ella helped with the kids.

Chapter Twenty-four

Saturday 19-01-19

Six days overdue. I was to be induced.

I had been doing hypnobirthing sessions with Sue on a regular basis, and we'd had lots of meetings while she kept a close eye on my mental health along with everything else. We would talk, she would give advice, but no-one had the answers as to how life was going to be after the baby was born or whether Mr R was going to be there for me. She made me realise that I had to put myself first for the first time in years – not Mr R, not his family, not his expectations, not the kids. Me. I had to do this to safely deliver this little baby that I had fought for and protected for nine months. I was ready as I'd ever be.

I had made up my mind by that point that if Mr R wasn't going to be at the birth, I was all good to go do this alone. And I honestly meant it. It had been my choice to go ahead and have this baby, and my choice to do it alone.

I often wondered what people thought when they saw me at appointments, a woman in her mid-thirties alone. At the 4D scan, I made out that my partner had such a successful business that he had no time off – it was half true; I just missed out the bit where he was at home with his family! That was a technicality. At times like that, I felt sad and humiliated.

Going into labour alone, though, absolutely wasn't going to happen. Not on Vicki's watch! She had been outside the room when I'd had Reggie, so it was a running joke that if I was ever to have another, she would be there by hook or by crook.

My mum was there to have the kids; Ella wasn't far away from either me or the kids to help my mum; Sue was ready and waiting; I had my friends on call or on the end of a text; and of course, my aunt was there if I needed her. I was so lucky to be surrounded by such amazing and loyal people, such strong, incredible women! But sadly, Mr R was who I wanted, and who I thought at that time I needed.

The night before the induction day, my body was done. I was ready to pop, and the water infection was well and truly taking hold. Mum and I discussed whether Mr R would make it to the hospital. She never thought for one moment that he wouldn't, but she knew how much family meant to him and what an awful choice he had to make. It would have made things worse for him if his family ever found out that he had slipped out to see his child be born, then go home and eat his dinner.

Despite that, I hated just not knowing whether he would show up or not, and my psychic ability was all off for any answers!

My mum shared with me that my dad hadn't been at my birth and said it didn't matter if a father was there or not. She said it was more important how he behaved after the baby was born, and pointed out how my dad has been an amazing father and wasn't there to see me arrive, while my ex had been present at the birth of both Jasmine and Reggie but definitely wasn't an amazing father. She made it sound very simple, and the vision was set in my mind. He wasn't going to be there, and I accepted that. I thank my mum so much for that insight, which enabled me to stop the constant wandering around my mind… although I couldn't help but still have a little hope.

Vicki and I set off to the hospital with my hair blow-dried – thanks to Ella – my nails done, and a hospital bag that had only been packed the day before (I wasn't in denial at all, was

I?). When we were on our way, I tried to persuade Vicki to take me to a furniture shop, as I was sure I needed storage containers for something. It felt as though we were going on a day out, not having a baby that was going to change my life forever.

I was heading into becoming a single mum of three, with lots of explaining to do as the baby got older. And as we pulled into the hospital car park, the long-ago words of that Google search still haunted me.

Once I'd been checked into the ward, Vicki kept looking at me if I was mad! Why? Because I was still working, whilst further readings were being booked in! Not once did I say, 'Sorry, I'm out of the office as I'm having some time to have a baby today!' I just kept going. As always, my vision was to work hard, have my baby, and continue to build an empire for me and my (now) three bears.

Once I'd been settled in at the hospital, Vicki and I laughed a lot. We had so much stuff with us, from hot water bottles to an extension lead (which we got told off for). She must have done 50 runs up and down to the hospital shop getting anything I needed or wanted. Nothing was too much trouble; she was amazing. Even over the Christmas period leading up to my due date, she had stopped drinking alcohol and had announced that without a doubt she would put her Christmas dinner down to be there and hold my hand if need be.

At the start of my induction, she slept for most of the night in a chair, bless her heart, right by my side. As my contractions got stronger, I wandered around the corridors with the midwife asking me if I wanted pain relief, but I had my crystals and my positive thoughts. I completed my latest Netflix series on my phone, carried on doing my online readings, and just breathed my way through the pain that was coming thick and fast.

And where was Mr R?

He knew where I was. I had sent him a message saying the hospital were keeping me in. We'd had an awkward conversation that morning, as I knew I was being induced but I couldn't talk about it to him. He didn't even know my due date. That probably sounds like a strange decision not to tell him, but I didn't want to add even more pressure to the complicated web of lies we were tangled in. With or without him, I was doing everything I could to keep going.

At one point I did send a message to say Vicki was with me but asked him to come to the hospital if he could. His reply was that he had a bit of a cold. A cold? Honestly, it was the worst thing he could have said. I'm sure you're thinking what a dickhead he was! I did, too! He wasn't a bad person and I'm not making excuses for him, but I had always known the score. I didn't hear from him again that night.

I was attached to a monitor for a big chunk of the night, so sitting in one place I continued running my business to get through the hours. At one point a lovely lady next to my bed was in so much pain, bless her, that I sat with her with my crystals in my hand and talked her through the contractions. It was baby number four for her, so she was a pro at this, but she wasn't coping. Vicki again looked at me like I was mad, but I felt drawn to help the lady if I could. Plus, her husband was always ordering fast food and cheesy chips, so we weren't going to miss out on that!

Later, the same lovely lady, Lucy, and her husband – the ones who met my baby before anyone else – sat in the audience of my live mediumship show when my life had changed so much.

The next morning, the pain was coming fast. Vicki was down on yet another shop run, it was 8.15am, and my waters started to go. My babies have all been born quickly, and the midwife wanted me on labour ward ASAP, so we rushed through. Vicki arrived soon after with her what-did-I-miss? face on, and loaded up with all the bags. I still find it hilarious when I remember it, as we looked like we were staying for a week. But Vicki is the queen of snacks, so we had everything we could need – and more!

I was in the birthing pool, well and truly into my labour, while the healthcare worker who was still bringing bags with Vicki was moaning and telling us off about an extension lead. It's a story we still talk about to this day! Did they not realise I had a business to run? I was multitasking! I wanted to punch her, if I'm honest. I was pushing a baby out, for God's sake!

Vicki called Sue and, like the angel she was, she came. Throughout the half hour I was in the birthing pool, I had my eyes closed the whole time. My hypnobirthing came into play, and I listened to the voice of Sue taking me up the hill and down the hill with the waves (aka contractions). At the top of the hill were Jasmine and Reggie in my happy place. They were there waiting for me, the sun was shining, and there was a picnic. I don't know why there was a picnic but there was, and my nan was there. She was present in that room as if she was on earth and on that hill, just like my children, Vicki, and Sue.

I briefly thought about the kids' dad in moments of labour, as he had been there in my only experience of labour in the past, but it didn't put me off the job in hand. Yep, childbirth came flooding back. It was painful and it was like my body being ripped in half, but I focused on Sue's voice and kept my vision.

Still no word from Mr R.

Chapter Twenty-five

Forty-five minutes later, and with one final push, my baby – Angel number three – was in my arms. I was free! The light switched on, and nothing was dark any longer.

I felt the torment, the torture, the emotional weight I had been carrying for nine long months just fade away. SHE was here in my arms, with loads of black hair, olive skin, and a pure combination of my three favourite people!

I lent on Sue, and I said out loud, 'I'm free.' Vicki held my hand, sobbing proudly, and I cried.

I had done it!

The power of the mind and the vision is such a powerful thing: if you believe you will receive.

All the cracks that had started to appear in my heart suddenly healed, and all the breath I had been holding finally released from my lungs. Nothing else mattered in that moment. SHE was the light of my life.

But then panic filled the room. I was bleeding, my placenta was stuck, and I was rushed into surgery. For the first time in years, I had to remove my necklace that Mr R had bought me. It was very special to me and always made me feel close to him when he wasn't around. I felt so disconnected from him anyway, that this was almost the last straw. But I felt this was the universe reminding me that no matter what, I was strong enough to deal with anything that life threw at me!

I desperately wanted him to appear, but he didn't.

Yet I'm grateful now that I did it alone with my strength and my vision. I also kept my promise that I would do it with or without him.

You may or not have worked out that 20th January, 2019 – the day my baby was born – was in fact... a SUNDAY!

Twenty-four hours later, I messaged him with a simple photo of me and the baby together, and he replied, 'It's a girl, isn't it?'

I was tired of guessing how this would go, so I let it be. I didn't even reply.

Vicki offered to reach out to him multiple times, but I didn't want my bubble to burst, and I had no energy for him. My kids were all that mattered, and my business.

It took four long days for him to come and meet her at my house. It was awkward and surreal, but we got through it. She screamed the whole time, but it gave him an opportunity to hold her. I could see he felt the connection, but he was torn.

Slowly, he began to spend more time with us again and he began to do his routine days. She was still a secret from his family, but she was the completeness of mine. Jasmine and Reggie adored her more than I think they ever knew possible, and there we were, a family of four: me, Jasmine, Reggie, and Arabella.

Mr R didn't engage in naming her or anything official, which was selfish, but again, he always put HIS family first. As far as I was concerned, he would always have his place with us when he was ready. But would he ever be ready?

Fast forward a year.

We had moved house again (four months after Arabella was born).

I was relieved, because although it was only five minutes down the road, it had a whole different vision than the previous house where I'd felt so unhappy.

And so much had changed. The baby was now one, and Jasmine was in an incredible secondary school. My whole reason for moving to that town was still positive for their education, and in the new house I felt better than ever in myself, the way I looked, and my whole being.

Yes, Mr R was still at his home, and I was still getting just my few evenings. But our baby had her dad for the time he was there, and he adored her!

Everything had turned around in many ways, but the feeling of being on the outside of someone else's marriage still lurked in the shadows of my life.

I took the three kids on holiday on my own, back to my happy place in Lanzarote, to the same hotel I loved, the moon on the balcony, the sea, and freedom. And again, we met some wonderful people. I used the same story of Mr R and our 'unblended family', but I had changed.

My business had gone from strength to strength, and I was choosing to raise three kids on my own, because the man I loved had to put his own family first. I never stopped working, and I never stopped the vision. Although it sounds the same, it really wasn't. Now I was able to stand on my own two feet, comfortably supporting my children and their needs and more, providing for them, and making a difference to other people's lives.

Arabella was such an easy baby, and she fitted into our lives like she was always meant to. I loved every second of having a baby again and enjoyed her so much, probably because I was that bit older and I had my own house, my own way, with no-one telling me what to do, as it had been with my previous babies. It was as though she had always been part of us.

She was a gift, my Angel. And she saved us all in so many ways. The light in our lives.

We were *never* going to have a 'normal' family life, but everything had finally calmed down… until that dreadful morning when I found myself collapsed on the floor in the ensuite when he told me it was over.

Chapter Twenty-six

As I mentioned earlier, I scraped together the last piece of money I could to try and piece my life back together with the help of the Unconscious Mind Therapy, and UMT helped to reaffirm that I was being everything I wanted to be and so much more.

I still don't know how I managed to function whilst looking after three kids when I was at my lowest, but my UMT session played a huge role in changing my life from the day I had my treatment onwards.

Even when Mr R's family found out, even when the world knew we'd had a child together whilst he was still living there, I found a way to move forward with the tools from UMT.

A productive talk therapy, UMT aims to resolve the problem that's holding you back in your life, rather than focussing directly on the problem itself. Unlike most therapies that often take months, if not years, to see improvement, UMT results are instantaneous. You can feel the positive effect from the very first session!

And I did! It changed my whole way of thinking. Although I'd had the foundations of placing the right thought into my mind to become the reality,

I never knew the depth of the power of my own thought process.

UMT focuses on the recovery rather than the content of the issue that is blocking your journey in your life, preventing you from moving forward, and reaching your full potential.

It can help you change past thoughts, feelings, limiting beliefs, and patterns, and give you an incredible mindset which results in you creating the vision to be happy, focussed, and in control.

From that first and only session of UMT, my life changed. I was becoming the businesswoman I had been in awe of when I thought about Vicki's mum. I was becoming someone my children could be proud of, able to fully provide for them with no fear or doubts.

I never give up; I never stop; and my desire to make my business the best is my second love, next to my children.

I took up the UMT therapist's offer of joining the live performance, and once that was safely under my belt, I created a vision of a solo stand-up show in a theatre. But not just any theatre – the same one I had sat in years before watching a friend perform magic. I often think back to that moment when I first walked into that theatre and sat watching my friend's show, and somehow I knew then that it had a special feeling. It was a feeling that never left me, and whenever I imagined myself performing my mediumship, it was always in that theatre. The vintage surroundings provided such a friendly and humble atmosphere, and that's what I wanted to share with anyone who chose to come and spend the evening with me.

So, just three months after that UMT session, and still not knowing what my future was with Mr R, I was ready to take to the stage – alone!

I did everything myself that week leading up to the show, every detail of the production, from arranging people to do certain jobs to support me, to choosing the kids their outfits. It was a huge learning curve for me, particularly as I was continuing to deliver readings within my business and raise my three children whilst the world of Mr R and me had spun in so many circles.

On the night of the sold-out event, it was pouring with rain and Storm Dennis was out in force. I was so apprehensive about whether people would even bother to venture out of their homes, but it was a sell-out. Wow!

People had paid to come and watch me perform my very first ever live solo event in a theatre, and that meant so much to me. My children sat and watched me work, delivering heartfelt messages from lost loved ones in spirit to those on earth, making a difference by helping people heal a little bit of grief in their hearts, giving them some light in their lives – just as spirit had done for me the whole of my children's little lives.

Showing them that they could be proud was everything to me.

In the days leading up to the big night, I had spirit stepping forward to reach out. They knew who was coming to the event before I did, so they were prepared and grabbing their link to earth to make their connection through me.

The heat I felt around my body from spirit coming in closer and closer was comforting me, knowing that I wasn't going to be let down by the other side.

For the whole hour before the show, my aunt sat with me while I paced back and forth. I had to keep moving as I prepared to connect with spirit, because it encourages the energy to build. My aunt's constant reassurance also kept me confident that I was going to do well, and I trusted my vision that the event would be a huge success.

I always make my promise to the spirit world that I will work to the highest of my ability, and in turn I ask for strong detailed messages from them. Not too much to ask for, eh?

Seconds before stepping out into the packed auditorium, my aunt held my hand and gave it a squeeze. And the barman to my left looked at me with kind eyes and said quietly, 'You got this.' I don't think he ever knew at that moment what a difference he made to the seconds before I was called on stage.

The Greatest Showman soundtrack 'This Is Me' blasted through the whole theatre as my chosen entry music. Spirit were ready, and my audience waited, including my kids, my mum, my friends who had watched me struggle throughout the challenges in my life, and clients I had gained during the build-of my business. The adrenaline zipped through my body, the energy building, and I could feel my amazing Nan in spirit come close. I could feel her pushing me to go and be the person I had truly become, and I knew she was proud of me.

I took a deep breath and instinctively took off my shoes to perform barefoot. It was a strange thing to do, as I'm very much a shoe girl, but it felt right at that moment and there was no time for second guessing. I heard my compere announce, 'Ladies and gentlemen, please welcome your medium for this evening, Amy Fleckney!' *Shit, that's me!* was the only thought that went through my mind.

As I stepped out onto the stage, like a film clip in my brain I saw that girl from the caravan struggling to survive in a world of single parenting, raising her children with hope and a vision, the very same girl who had fallen in love and created a world with Mr R that maybe no-one would ever understand or accept. She was right there in my heart. I carry her everywhere, and I owe it to her to remember her strength and continue to succeed. And that's exactly what I did that night. It was an incredible show for so many reasons, from the messages I delivered to the gratitude I received. I wasn't just existing any more; I was finally living the life that I love.

Change can happen in an instant, and you always have a choice, even when you feel like you don't. It's right there, always in your mind, to have the power to make the change.

Chapter Twenty-seven

Two years later

I wake up in the night, and he is there. I wake up again a little later, and he is still there. Phew! The relief I feel inside me is overwhelming.

It's so strange to wake up during the night and see him lying next to me, when I think back to the endless nights of waking alone, panicking, trying to find the strength to get through another day of making our relationship work and not letting the elephant in the room take away our moments of happiness.

But not any more.

We are now at the end of Covid Lockdown 2021 – a time Mr R spent with us in our bubble to make sure that he could see Arabella. We did all the normal stuff I had once visualised, and waking up next to him in the night was just one of the simple things I promised I would never take for granted.

Finally, we were having the 'what are we having for dinner?' and 'what are we doing tomorrow?' conversations, and I had to pinch myself to trust that it wasn't a dream. But let's be honest, we definitely weren't running into the sunset together any time soon, and I had to realise that this new arrangement was going to be a whole journey of its own.

You will have realised that staying away from me and trying to make his marriage work didn't work out as he had planned back in 2019.

Living with us was temporary for Covid, and how he finally made his choice to be true to himself and others is not my story to tell, but I knew from now on I was no longer going to be feeling that dread of him going home, or that fear of the unknown.

During this journey, I struggled with resentment, anger, and my mental health again. Clients often ask me how I can be so positive ALL the time, but I have to tell them I'm not! My explanation is that mental health is like an ex-boyfriend knocking at the door. You know you have to close the door to continue moving forward, but you're always slightly curious to hear what they have to say. I'm not always positive, and I still suffer some days where the fog will try to come back.

As the Christmas of 2021 approached, I was struggling to eat, and my tummy was so sore I was spending hours in the bathroom, completely doubled over in pain. In my head I was questioning why this was happening again.

I was stressed because I was supporting the love of my life trying to rebuild his life after his whole world, as he knew it, came crashing down and he finally had to walk away from his family.

I had worked for the previous three years building my business, reading for people all over the world at all hours of the day and night. Some days I wouldn't even go to bed because I would be reading all night, or I would be functioning on very little sleep whilst continuing to raise my three kids.

I wanted Mr R to feel loved and looked after, to know that I was going to support him no matter what challenges we would face, that I was by his side, and that I was never the 'nice shirts and nights out' girl I was made out to be. I was hard on myself constantly through this time, but so grateful all the time for the fact I could open my eyes in the night and see him there.

But my belly was bad... so I went back to my amazing doctor who ran some bloods. One week before Christmas, I was waiting for my results to come through and the receptionist at the surgery said I had to see the doctor to discuss them. I knew that wasn't normal. Usually, they just say, 'Tests all clear, no further action.'

While I was waiting to speak to my doctor, and quietly freaking out about what could be wrong, I got a call from the hospital to confirm that I was being booked in for an emergency scan three days before Christmas.

What was going on? Why was I being booked in within days without any explanation from my doctor? I was chasing everyone I could speak to, but no-one had answers, only that I had to speak to the doctor himself. When I finally got hold of him, he said he wanted to speak to me in person rather than on the phone. I was way beyond worrying by that stage, then he told me, 'Your ovarian cancer marker is slightly raised.' I froze on the spot in my kitchen and sobbed, but no sound came out.

My doctor said, 'Please come and see me so that I can re-assure you this will be ok. The marker is only slightly high, so the likelihood of it being cancer would be slim.' He assured me he just didn't want to take any chances, and that's why the emergency scan had been arranged.

Despite his assurances, the news hit me like a bus, and my mind started spinning about how I couldn't tell my children, and how I didn't want to lose my hair. It's awful to think like that, but I was so frightened. You never expect to be told news like that. I had worked with so many clients in similar situations, but I didn't have the answers, and certainly couldn't reassure myself.

Mr R, with his usual laid-back attitude, seemed unfazed by the news and kept saying I was going to be ok. He couldn't engage in anything to do with the fact I might be unwell, but I felt so alone. Yet again, Mum came to stay so I could go to the scan and not worry my kids so close to Christmas.

I really needed Mr R to step up.

In so many ways he does, and it would be cruel for me to paint a picture of him being heartless, because he isn't. I know I'm his world and we have come so far in our relationship, but I needed him to be emotionally involved with his reassurance for me. He isn't the best with words, and he was struggling with the battle he had ahead of him, trying to rebuild relationships with his children, and to get used to a whole new way of life.

Jenny sat outside the scan, like she would back in the days of meeting me on the school run after a long night. And thankfully, the results came back clear.

To this day, I am still working with my doctor to get to the bottom of why my belly suffers like it does. But since my UMT, I know and appreciate that energy has to flow, and that any negative emotion building up in my body will go somewhere. For me, it's my belly. I wonder where yours goes?

The health scare and the fact that I was holding our situation together while he was going through a complex divorce, was tough for me. I felt so much resentment build up, as Mr R never really knew how hard it was, and it made me angry that he struggled to express his gratitude to me for always standing by him – even when it was at the cost of my own health.

I don't doubt you're thinking, *FFS, Amy, why are you not happy? You wanted him, and you got him. You got your 'normal'! Be happy.*

And I was 'happy', but life is never as simple as that. I'd gone through so much to get to this stage, but I was so grateful I'd never have to watch him go on another holiday again whilst I waved him goodbye with a heavy heart.

Happiness, though, comes with the scars of the past for me. And in this case, it was questions I could finally ask Mr R that I had always been too scared to voice before: Why didn't you make the choice yourself to leave? Why didn't you come the day Arabella was born? Why did you wait for someone to take the choice away from you to do the right thing, making this so much harder for everyone involved?

Again, he didn't have the answers…

Google's advice to 'stay clear of married men' was probably right in the grand scheme of things. But not once did Google say that as the 'other woman' if you finally get your happy ending, the feeling of never being good enough for however many years would creep up on you at some point. And that feeling was creeping up on me.

I found myself feeling distant from Mr R, which was crazy considering this was what I had been wanting for so long. My mental health started going backwards, and I felt like all those years had done something to me, something I couldn't describe. A rolling ball of resentment towards him started to snowball – the opposite of anything I ever thought I could feel – and there I was like a raging bull. It wasn't a great look for me; I don't suit it. I love calm and tranquillity.

On top of all these feelings and thoughts, I was still working all the hours to keep building my empire, with no structure for times or days, and just suppressing my thoughts and feelings again to make sure everyone was happy.

We had an unbearable shock during lockdown when Arabella was diagnosed with juvenile arthritis in both her feet. It was heart-breaking to know my ray of light was suffering in so many ways, and we had a long battle to get her seen by the right people and to access the right care. She was struggling to walk, her feet and ankles were swollen all the time, she looked a yellowy colour, and she would hum to herself a lot. I later learned that this is a common pain management control, as the humming causes gentle vibration which eases the pain.

I felt numb, and still feel numb. She is now on medication that I have to administer to her by injection, and it's taken two years to stabilise her condition, but she still gets poorly from immune suppressant meds, and her chest infections and endless temperatures are a way of life for us now. Hospital visits have become so regular that the A&E department knows me by my first name.

Despite all her struggles, she is still the happy ray of light she was when she was first placed in my arms, and she inspires me every day with her strength. With everything we have been through, I will never take my health or having two other healthy children for granted.

During this time, opportunities were going from strength to strength within my business. The life-changing experience I had with UMT encouraged me to study to be a UMT practitioner at the UMT Academy, and I now help clients of my own change their lives with the power of Unconscious Mind Therapy. I was invited to be part of an incredible collaboration book to share a chapter of my story, and this experience again changed my life, meeting other women who have been through diverse and heart-breaking trauma in their lives. We shared our stories in *The Girls Who Refused to Quit (Volume 3)*, and I also contributed a chapter for a follow-up book called *Beautifully Broken*.

This is definitely when my healing started to come, My resentment began to fade and the torment in my mind settled. I was now in a position to really help people, and Mr R was right beside me as my biggest cheerleader – just as he had been that day when he stood with me at the Jesus Christ statue in Lisbon, and again when he held out his hand to me at my nan's grave.

Despite all the shit, he is there for me in his own way, and I am learning again to be in our relationship without fear or doubt.

Mr R makes me a better version of me when I remember how far we have come, and we have a soul connection that no resentment, anger, or challenge could destroy.

I have finally learned to accept that life as we know it can change, and UMT has given me the power to respond better and to make these moments more manageable. With the fog clearing, I'm able to believe that the visions in my mind have no limits.

Chapter Twenty-eight

July 2022

I had a flashback to walking into my first UMT session: scared, afraid, broken, and uncertain of the future.

Who would have thought then that three years later I would experience one of the proudest days of my life? Surrounded by my close friends and family, and with Arabella watching in the arms of Mr R, I cut the ribbon held by Jasmine and Reggie to officially open my very own Spiritual and Unconscious Mind Therapy centre.

Amy Fleckney World had finally arrived!

I'd be lying if I said that everything is rosy in Amy Fleckney world, because it's not. I place immense pressure on myself to make sure I deliver the ultimate experience, whether that's through spirit or UMT. And I am still juggling three children and supporting Mr R through his challenges, which still haven't had closure.

I made a promise the day I cut the ribbon that everyone who walks through the doors of Amy Fleckney World will always walk back out of them with a feeling of change for the better. And I have big visions for the future, even if I'm not entirely sure of how they will come to life.

But one thing I know for sure is that when worlds collide, it doesn't mean it's the end. It's an invitation to create a whole new beginning.

To be continued…

Amy Heckney's Inspirational Insight

Some of the positive steps I took to move forward with my life were...

to not feel ashamed to ask for help. It's totally okay to need support and guidance, whether that be from friends or a professional.

It's not a sign of weakness; it's a sign of your strength and integrity to want better in life for yourself and for the special people around you.

If you are going through any similar challenges, I want you to know...

nothing is impossible, nothing is out of reach, and dreams do become reality.

When people say you can't, prove them wrong. Because, trust me, you can!

Finding a home in your heart that will always keep you safe, a secure place that makes you realise how loved you are, will intuitively guide you to where you need and deserve to be.

In my case, it was my children.

We all have a gut feeling... trust it, and never let anyone take your power away. Live life on your terms, without fear or doubt. At times it may feel relentless, and it might not be easy, but I can promise you it will be worth it

I wished I had known…

the power of the mind and how creating a vision, a thought, and a feeling, really does become your reality.

I learned to place the correct information into my brain and focus on what I really wanted for my life and how I saw it in my mind, rather than repetitive thoughts of what I *didn't* want.

Visualising is the key to creating a better life, and it all starts with you in your thoughts.

I found the switch in my hand to turn the light back on… I just didn't realise I was holding it the whole time.

Little did I know my ability to connect to spirit would support me and my children to a better life, I would be helping others to heal, and I'd become the businesswoman I had visualised becoming.

It was inside of me the whole time.

Unconscious Mind Therapy

Unconscious mind therapy (UMT) is a productive talk therapy that aims to resolve the problem that's holding you back in your life, rather than focusing directly on the problem.

Unlike most therapies that often take months, if not years to see improvement, UMT results are instantaneous, You will feel the positive effects from the very first session!

UMT focuses on the recovery rather than the content of the issue that is blocking your journey, preventing you from moving forward, and reaching your full potential.

UMT can help you change past thoughts, feelings, limiting beliefs, and patterns, and give you an incredible mindset resulting in you creating the vision to be happy, focused, and in control of any challenges you face.

The success Unconscious Mind Therapy can bring to you, whether it be in business or your personal life, is endless. It can help with:

Depression

Anxiety

Trauma

Phobias

Relationship issues

Addiction

Blocked paths

Moving forward

Grief

Weight loss

Quitting smoking

And so much more.

Helping you to live a life you love.

To find out more, or book your session, email Amy Fleckney: info@amyfleckneymediumship.co.uk

An overview of the clairs

The Clairs are types of psychic abilities using your five senses. When I connect to my ability, my mind and body become flooded with: thoughts, feelings, images, sounds, tastes, and smells.

Clairvoyance means clear seeing. This is when visions past, present, and future are shown through our mind's eye (third eye), much like a daydream.

Clairaudience means clear hearing. This is when we hear words, sounds, or music in our own mind's voice rather than our ears. Spirit may be able to create sound.

Clairsentience means clear feeling. This brings feeling of a person's spirit's emotions, or feeling another's physical pain. Many of us are clairsentient without consciously being aware of it. When we get a 'gut' feeling – positive or negative – about someone we just met, or when we get an 'unsettled feeling' for no apparent reason, we may be tuning into the emotional energy of a person or a spirit around us.

Clairalience means clear smelling. This is being able to smell certain odours that don't have any kind of physical source. Spirit may present the smell of cooking if they were a keen cook, offering the smell of a favourite dish, for example.

Clairgustance means clear tasting. This is the ability to taste something that isn't actually there. This experience often comes when a passed loved one is attempting to communicate a memory or association which they have with a particular taste.

Claircognizance means clear knowing. This is when we have knowledge of people or events that we would not normally know about. Spirit provides us with truths that simply come into our minds. The biggest source of evidence from spirit comes from claircognizance.

Acknowledgments

To Mr R, there are no words to express how grateful I am that our paths crossed and you came into my life.

Through the twists & turns we have faced, what we have found in each other is rare.

You are my soul mate. You help me to be the best version of me, and I'm a better person because you're in my life.

I love you with all my heart.

To my parents, you are the two most consistent people in my life. You never let me down, and I'm so lucky to have you as my mum and dad.

To Cassandra Welford, my author mentor, publisher, and most of all my friend.

You have given me life-changing opportunities that I will treasure forever, and you truly are one of a kind.

The Universe had bigger plans for us the day we met, and the magic in our friendship I will treasure for ever.

People don't give a sh*t about a lot, but you ALWAYS do!

Thank you for being my WW, my soul sister, and always believing in me.

Watch out, world, we are coming for you!

To my Auntie Janni, thank you for supporting me to be the best medium I can be. You will forever be my teacher and my friend.

To Robert Heisee for helping me find the real Amy Fleckney again.

To my beautiful friends – you know who you are.

You have all played a role in my healing, my journey, and you're the family I got to choose.

You saved me when I struggled to save myself.

Thank you won't ever be enough

My nan in spirit world, thank you for being my guide. And my little nan on earth, thank you for being you. Xxx

About the Author

Amy (with the long red hair), who lives in Essex, England, is well known as a fighting spirit and an incredibly hard worker.

She has been described as fiercely loyal, kind, and someone with their feet firmly flat on the ground.

She can usually be found working long hours as a renowned psychic medium and Unconscious Mind Therapist, running her spiritual centre in Essex. Committed to her clients and working with spirit, she simultaneously juggles the joys of being a full-time mum to her three beautiful children and life with her partner, Mr R.

Despite the hardships she has faced, she has always remained sedulous and now finds herself with a growing following in the UK, America, and Australia, including celebrity clients, and continues her journey as a stage platform medium.

In the free time she has, she enjoys spending time with her parents and her close friends.

Amy's goal is to help as many people as possible to live a life they love.

What real clients say about Amy...

"Amy has such a beautiful energy and accuracy with her readings, she never fails to hit the spot."

Jaqueline, Nottingham

"Amy is eerily accurate. The world is a better place because of people like Amy."

Hillary, Pennsylvania

"Never met a lady like Amy. I entered her room a curled-up mess, and after a one-hour session with her I left with my head held high and the courage to take my life forward in a way I never felt possible.

"Amy didn't just leave me there. She messaged me to see how I'm going… that was priceless. Her heart is pure gold. One amazing, clever lady."

Dawn, Hertfordshire

Connect with Amy Fleckney

Website: www.amyfleckneymediumship.co.uk

Instagram: amyfleckneymedium

Email: info@amyfleckneymediumship.co.uk

Facebook: Amys Mediumship and psychic readings

Facebook group: Amys psychic mediumship reviews & more

TikTok: amyfleckneymediumship

Amy would appreciate you leaving a review for *When Worlds Collide* on Amazon.

Amy Heckney's Books

The Girls Who Refused to Quit (Volume 3) – Chapter 4

Beautifully Broken – Chapter 4

When Worlds Collide

All titles are available on Amazon

What you think you become,
What you feel you attract,
What you imagine you create.

Buddha

Lightning Source UK Ltd.
Milton Keynes UK
UKHW021838010223
416318UK00006B/25